96 TEARS

ROBERT MONTI

Gotham Books

30 N Gould St.
Ste. 20820, Sheridan, WY 82801
https://gothambooksinc.com/

Phone: 1 (307) 464-7800

© 2025 *Robert Monti*. All rights reserved.

No part of this book may be reproduced, stored in a retrieval system, or transmitted by any means without the written permission of the author.

Published by Gotham Books (April 11, 2025)

ISBN: **979-8-3485-3637-4** (H)
ISBN: **979-8-3485-3880-4** (P)
ISBN: **979-8-3485-3881-1** (E)

Because of the dynamic nature of the Internet, any web addresses or links contained in this book may have changed since publication and may no longer be valid.

The views expressed in this work are solely those of the author and do not necessarily reflect the views of the publisher, and the publisher hereby disclaims any responsibility for them.

Table of Contents

Age Of Innocence	1
Time to Grow Up	24
Ping Pongs	35
Rose Colored Glasses	43
Only the Beginning	48
The Devil Shows His Face	52
Shadows	57
Divine Intervention	60
Never A Dull Moment	64
Different Direction	67
Voice From The Past	71
Back To Reality	73
Purple People Eater	81
Hell House	86
A Time to Contemplate	97
96 Tears	103
Starting Over	108
One Summer Knight	126
Summer Knights	135
The Back Stabbers	143
You're My Favorite	147
A Prayer For Sunshine	153
Epiphany	155
Surrounded By Angels	159
Broken Promises	162
Judas	170
Icing On The Cake	178
Beginning Of The End	185
Starting Over	195
Summary	199
About the Author	200

Dedication

To all my Guardian Angels who have watched over and guided me

To my friends and family that inspired me over the years

In Loving Memory of my dad

Carmine Montuori

the most influential person of my life

and the greatest man I have ever known

Special thanks to my sister MaryAnn Miano in co-writing and whose endless energy and zest for life has inspired us all

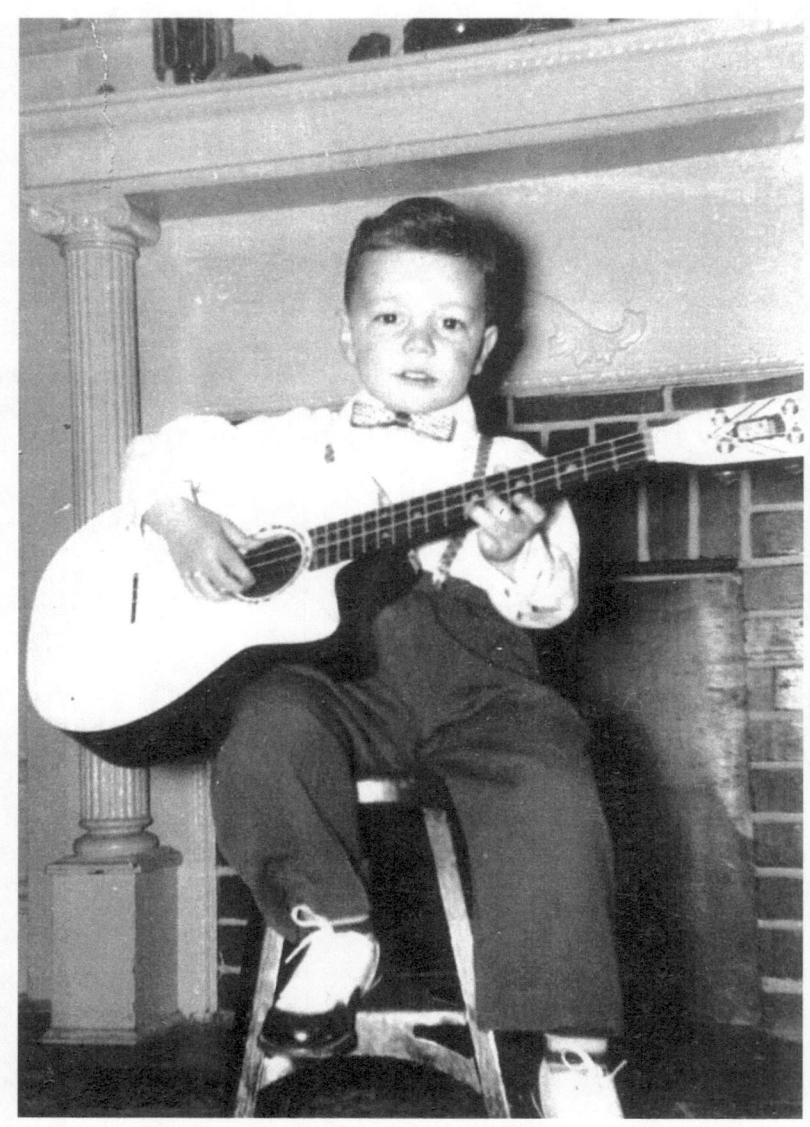

*Bobby Monti
Circa 1953*

AGE OF INNOCENCE

In perhaps one of the greatest eras in history, an era of booming prosperity and productivity, a time that gave birth to television, rock & roll, and rocket ship automobiles, there I was, being brought up in black and white. The time of Leave It to Beaver, Ozzie and Harriet, and Father Knows Best, a simpler time and place, where people still had ideals, morals, and character. At least, it seemed so.

Every night as I said my prayers, I would repeat a special prayer to my guardian angel that was on a wooden plaque that hung above my bed:

Angel of God, my guardian dear, to whom His love commits me here. Ever this day be at my side, to light and guard, to rule and guide. Amen.

Then I would close my eyes and my mind would drift to thoughts of my day and my excitement for tomorrow.

It was 1958 in Gravesend, Brooklyn, a neighborhood that enjoyed every popular fad and craze the times had to offer. The only sad note was that the Dodgers had left for Los Angeles. It seemed like that was the topic to talk about in Brooklyn for quite some time. The culture of the day was already starting to mark my psyche, an indelible mark to this day that defines who I am.

I can think back and still see images that left lasting impressions. My friends and

I would be standing inside the corner candy store deciding if we could afford to buy a "Pense Pinky" ball for the stick ball game we were about to have, when suddenly droves of girls with their saddle shoes and pleated skirts and pony tails came marching in for soda fountain treats. The junior high across the street had just let out. Wow! That time already. Well, you know we delayed our game-playing just to watch the girls.

Then the music started. You never knew where it was coming from, but it was always there, always great. We heard it in the jukebox, the disk changer at the counter, or somebody's transistor radio. I was impressed. I had to get myself one of those. I could listen to everything anytime I wanted.

There were images I had already stored in my mind, of roller skating and the crowd of kids singing "Goody Goody" by Frankie Lymon. Certain songs just seemed to become sing-a-longs, like "Personality" by Lloyd Price. At night back in those days, it seemed like every family was out on their porch steps socializing as the gang would play tag running between cars.

Then we'd all pause by someone's stoop and sing with the Maguire Sisters "Sugar in the Morning, Sugar in the Evening." The whole era was all about the music. We had Elvis and rock and roll and the group sound that emanated from everywhere. Whatever we heard was great, and we wanted to hear it over and over again.

One day my friend Buzzy thought it would be a cool thing if we became a street gang. The whole crowd agreed, myself included. Somehow he had come across decals of flaming skulls, which became our insignia. "Hot Heads" became our name. We were cool even though we were just kids, and as they say nowadays, grease was the word!

As time went by, we grew to be more mischievous. We pulled all kinds of nonsense, mostly amongst ourselves. One thing I can say, as I look back, is we never hurt anyone, except maybe ourselves and other kids. We found a place to hang out. My friend Ricky had an uncle who owned a bar on Avenue U.

Ricky said his uncle would let us stay in the backyard behind the bar as long as we stayed out of trouble. Something we never did, but never got caught at. Guys and girls were included. Our hangout became known as The Shadow Door. We transformed the name from the catering hall at the entrance of the alley, known as The Chateau D'or.

We used to rumble with a couple of other gangs in an empty lot behind our hangout.

It stretched from East 19th Street to behind an apartment complex on Ocean Avenue. One gang in particular from the projects seemed to become a routine battle for us every week. We were obsessed with beating each other up. It seemed nobody ever won and no one ever lost. It always ended on a "too be continued" episode. My days with the gang were starting to become numbered. Some of the adults in the building behind were becoming irate with the constant commotion, plus they were using the lot to park their cars.

One day as we were starting to congregate, a number of adult men came down to the lot and tried to grab as many of us as they could. Before we realized what was happening, most everyone had scattered, but Ricky and I were caught by some big Jewish rabbi that dragged us both by the collar into the building. To be honest we were scared, because this guy acted like he wanted to kill us. Ricky told me, "Bobby, relax he's a rabbi," as if that would keep him from hurting us.

Well the guy threw us into the elevator and slapped us around pretty good, including banging our heads against the elevator walls. He led us into his apartment and badgered us for information about the rest of our friends that got away. We weren't rats.

That was code on the streets.

We finally gave up our mothers' names and phone numbers. I rattled out "Nightingale 6 5521." We didn't know what this guy was capable of, and he refused to let us leave until our folks came to get us. Both moms showed up, and were very upset with what we told them happened. Somehow the rabbi seemed to make light of it all. Our moms bought it. Adults did that back then. They didn't seem to question other adults, just took them at their word. Needless to say, we were banned from the empty lot. Of course another lecture ensued when I got home, this time from my father, "Stay out of there! You ought to know better!" Then he asked me when I was going to learn to stay out of trouble and that I should go practice my guitar.

I was taking guitar lessons from my grandfather, Joe Monte. He was a professional musician, played Vaudeville, and toured the country with numerous big bands. I, of course, was trying to not disappoint. But my musical talents would surface later in other areas. I tried the best I could to stay away from the empty lot and just hang out at the Shadow Door.

We'd enter and exit from the front of the alley. Then suddenly one day a mini trailer appeared in front of the lot on the East 19th Street side. Wow, with this came the brain storm for entrepreneurship. My friends and I found a way of getting through the back fence behind the small Key Food store on Avenue U. It was a gold mine of empty bottles—1 and 2 cent deposit bottles! So we'd swipe bottles from the back of the store, crawl along under the trailer in the lot and back out onto 19 Street. We'd walk back into the store and cash in again!

This was very lucrative for a while. Until one day as I was crawling under the trailer, my arms full of bottles, when a voice rang out across the lot, "I see you, Bobby; I know what you are doing. I am going to tell your father." I stopped dead in my tracks. It was Mr. Salerno, from the first house after the lot. He didn't say another word, he just watched as I began to crawl backwards, putting the bottles back behind the store. I walked out, apologized to him, promised I'd never do it again. I put my head down, and walked out of the lot, sweating for the next year, that he wouldn't tell my father.

The final blow to my hang out with the Hot Heads came one day when I arrived home. My mother turned toward me as I was entering my room, "I want to talk to you!" I could tell by the sound of her voice I was in trouble. "What's this?" As she waved a black and white girlie book in my face.

I stood there, stunned. "Is this what you and your friends are doing at the Chateau D'or?" I looked at her stupidly and said, "How did you find out?"

"Never mind how I found out. You should be ashamed of yourself, and your friends, too! All the mothers are going to know about this! The girls are there too with this going on?"

"Yeah, but we don't let them see this stuff."

She continued, "I don't believe this. Your father works so hard to send you to parochial school. He's such a good man. Don't you want to grow up to be like your father? Believe in God, walk with your head held high, be proud of who you are?"

"Yes."

"I want you to be like your father." With that she hugged me. I felt so ashamed, so small. As she broke her embrace she said, "Now go to confession!"

Next week I was in church, as was the rest of my school class, making confession. The church and school were all one building. As I knelt by the guard rail in front of the alter saying my penance, my buddy Ricky kneeled down next to me and noticed me looking at the rack of prayer candles that people made offerings, lit, and prayed. There were dollar bills sticking half way out of the donation slot. Ricky looked at me, and I looked at him. We were both thinking the same thing. Ricky reached over, touched the bills looking at them, and then pushed them the rest of the way in. A voice rang out in the silence of the church. From a pew behind us, some kid we didn't know said, "Oooh I'm telling. You guys are stealing money."

We answered quickly, "We didn't take anything; we just pushed it in." Ricky and I returned to our classes, forgetting the incident until a girl came to our classroom, whispered something to the nun teaching our class, and left. Sister Margaret Mary announced our names and told Ricky and me to report to the principal's office. My heart jumped out of my chest and into my throat.

A most dreaded and feared thing to happen in life was about to happen. All the stories, the horrors, all raced through my head. The principal's office was a place in Catholic school that you never wanted to visit, especially if you were in trouble.

We entered the office door, which was open, and stood there. The room was empty. We didn't realize that the office was in two sections. Another wall and doorway separated the main room. Suddenly, waddling through the door was Sister Dorothy. She was the principal. She was huge and she was mean! She announced our names with her fleshy pink jowls jiggling as she approached us, "You boys know why you are here?"

"Yes sister, but we can explain. It's a mistake."

"I don't want to hear another word. You must learn to never touch anything that doesn't belong to you. Now, both of you put your hands in that bucket of water."

I'm thinking Oh God, what is she going to do to us? I can't even imagine, why put our hands in the water?

"Now put your hands on the edge of this desk." Next I see this yard stick in her hand. I knew what was coming and I grit my teeth. She started to swing the yard stick across our fingers. I'll never forget the sting as Ricky instinctively pulled his hands off the table after the first whack.

She yelled, "Get those hands back on that table, mister!" And again and again she whacked us. When she finally stopped, my hands were starting to bleed.

"Get back to your classes, and make sure I never see you here again."

"Yes sister," Ricky and I couldn't run fast enough. We got punished just for the thought of doing the wrong thing. Of course, we never told our folks anytime we were in trouble, because usually you'd just get clobbered again.

After the knuckle-busting experience, I was going to try my best at staying out of trouble. I was going to stay away from Ricky as much as I could. It wasn't his fault, but for some reason, whenever you were with him, trouble was sure to follow. I wasn't the only one that felt this way. The entire block of guys, and there were over a dozen of us, had the same experiences. Things got to the point where Ricky was resented by everyone in the gang. Finally, one day, he turned up waving a blade at everyone, defying them to do something about it. What happened next I guess he never expected.

At least six of us chased him down the block, took the knife and beat the daylights out of him. That was the last time I saw Ricky for quite some time.

The next day I'm riding my bike, baseball cards flapping between the spokes and little airplanes on the handle bars with their propellers spinning in the wind. It was such a cool bike. What was really cool, though, were the voices coming out of the hallway in the apartment building on the corner. I stopped outside the doorway to listen. A few of the older guys were singing. It sounded great—I loved it. I loved rock and roll. The group sound was rock and roll. Doo Wop was a term we weren't familiar with yet. Suddenly one of the guys opened the double glass door that graced the front of the foyer where they were singing, "Hey kid! Park your bike; come in here!"

I went inside. I thought it would be great to be up close. "Kid, "what's your

"Bobby,"

"Bobby, do you know why we sing in here?"

"No."

"Hit it guys." All sorts of ooh and ahhs came out. To this day it still gives me goose bumps. "Do you hear it, Bobby?

"Yeah, it sounds like its ringing."

"It's what we search for in a good hallway—ECHO. Do you hear the echo in here? You're going to help us out today. We are one guy short. I'm going to teach you what to do."

"Me?" I asked, nervously. I didn't know anything about singing except that I used to sing along to my records.

"Ok kid. Pay attention. I want you to do what I do. I'll give you your note." He hit an oooh. "Do that."

"Ooooh," I eeked out. It was awful and they let me know it. The guy behind me smacked me in the head,

"Listen to him, and do exactly that note—the same 'oooh' he does," pointing to his mouth, "ooooh."

"Ooooh." I got another smack in the head. Every time I messed up, they let me know about it. As you can imagine, I made sure I learned real fast. By the end of their session, I finally seemed to get it. I really liked it. When we hit harmony, it just did something to my insides. Besides that, the songs we were singing were so great- "Daddy's Home, In the Still of the Night, Long Lonely Night, Teardrops," all the classics.

"Good job, kid. Come in and sing with us whenever we are here."

I was so excited; I couldn't wait to do it again. I even decided to join the church choir that year. The biggest thrill was singing Christmas Eve in the church loft at Midnight Mass, knowing my folks and a lot of the neighbors were there to hear.

"I need you to watch your brother today." My mother would ask me for help, especially when my grandparents weren't going to be home. My mom's mother and father lived on the second floor. We called them Nani and Papa. They owned the house. My brother Ritchie was brain damaged at birth. He was a handful to take care of. My mom would say he was an angel of God, but also our cross to bear. I never did quite understand. I was the oldest of three boys. Next in line was my brother, Stevie, whom I spent most of my time teasing and fighting with. Ritchie was a challenge to keep occupied. He had the attention span of zero, so for me to keep him busy and entertained was a feat. Somehow I always managed to do it.

"When I get back, you can take a walk with Papa to the Bay." Mom knew I liked to walk with Papa to Sheepshead Bay, but she didn't know why. Papa loved to buy fresh fish off the boats. I liked that he always had chocolate Hershey bars in his pockets and always offered me one. The man knew everyone in the neighborhood. He liked to gab with some of them as we stopped along the way of wherever we were going.

Basically, the family was old-fashioned Italian. Papa tended to all the outside needs, including shopping for groceries, and Nani stayed home to take care of the house. Mom and Dad did the best they could raising us. Mom was a little on the neurotic side, always wanting for things to be perfect. With my brother Ritchie around, that was impossible. He actually destroyed the house—every piece of furniture and every molding had his teeth marks from where he chewed. Many a window he broke banging his head into the glass. It got so bad they had to put a helmet on him to keep him from splitting his head open.

Through all of this, mom still expected things to be perfect. If we had chores to do, and she didn't like the way things came out, she'd make us do it over again. Even when she checked my homework, if she didn't like it, she'd say "do it over." It was bad enough I tried to please the nuns at school. It seemed like whatever I did, it was never good enough.

Dad was a machinist and master mechanic. He did transmission and engine rebuilding. He used to take me to work with him. I helped him wash parts and any other errands he'd have me do. The first thing upon getting to work would find my father wiping the benches down, telling me to never work like these guys in the shop. "They're all slobs. Always be neat and clean, and your work will turn out good."

I used to like that my father would tell all the workers that I was his number one. He was proud of me, and it made me feel good. His boss drove in one day with a brand new '59 Caddy. It was the biggest, most beautiful car I'd ever seen. Dad noticed the look on my face, "You can have a car like that someday. You just have to knuckle down, study, and work hard." So with that, I saw an ad in my comic books to sell Christmas cards. With the money I made, I got my first transistor radio I was dying for.

Outside the house, life as a kid was fantastic. I grew up on a block with plenty of kids. Seemed like most of the boys lived on one side, and the girls on the other. No computers in those days, so we couldn't wait to get out of the house and play in the streets. Stickball, slap ball, punch ball, stoop ball, Johnny on the Pony, Ring a Levio, Skelly, basketball and street hockey--you name it, we did it. We used paint can lids before they invented Frisbees. I remember one time a blue painted lid went sailing over a garage roof right through someone's kitchen window while they were sitting there eating dinner. We heard the glass and the screams, and took off running. We had plenty of fun, sometimes at the expense of others.

As we headed into the 60s, life seemed to be becoming more serious. The years started marching on. My father would come down the basement steps, yell at me to lower the Victrola. I kept playing, "Please Love me Forever," by Kathy Jean and the Roommates, over and over, and he just couldn't take it anymore. It was a great song, but

Kathy Jean's voice was very piercing. My grandfather, Joe Monte, told me of Kathy Jean. He was in the studio when she was recording. He told me how amazed he was at her high voice.

Since the day the music died, I was becoming more conscious of people entering and leaving the world. Next thing I knew, Marilyn Monroe died, which was a shock to the country and still a mystery to this day.

That year seemed like death was in the air. A lot of old timers on the block were passing away. Every week somebody's front door was graced with a black and purple bow. Then things got close to home. Mr. Pampinella across the street from us died. He used to ask me to go up to the store and get him cigarettes. I never minded. I liked him. There were always a few cents in it for me. Imagine a kid could buy cigarettes back then without a question asked! I used to run errands for a lot of the old folks on the block. Sometimes they would give me a few cents, sometimes just a thank you. I didn't care. I just liked helping them. They would tell me stories of the neighborhood from years before. I loved listening and finding out interesting things.

Things hit home the day after Easter Sunday, 1962. I woke up extra early, and so did my brothers. It's amazing that you can sense when something is wrong. I walked out of my bedroom and down the hall. My father was just getting off the phone. I heard crying from upstairs. My father turned to us and said, "God took Papa home to Him this morning." I was devastated. It hit me like a ton of bricks that Papa wasn't going to be a part of my life anymore, that I would never see him again. You don't realize how much you care for someone until they are not in your life anymore. The only person that was able to console me was my grandma, my dad's mother. She had a soothing way about her. She held me while I was crying hysterically until I calmed down. I was starting to learn that life was rough. That Easter week felt like it would never end. The wake and the funeral was an entire week ordeal.

In the middle of all this anguish, I can still recall singing with my friend Buzzy and another friend Steven. He was a person also responsible for teaching me how to harmonize. Steven had an older sister, Carol, and I guess he was always listening to the music. He was into drums, but he was crazy about hitting harmony on the old songs. He seemed to be obsessed with "Teardrops," by Lee Andrews and the Hearts, and the Quotations' "Imagination." Steven said he had seen

The Quotations singing on the street corner outside Dubrow's Restaurant on Kings Highway and was crazy about them ever since. Another song he wanted to sing repeatedly was "Echo" by The Emotions.

My sister MaryAnn was born in September of '62. That was a thrill for the family. I was very excited. It fulfilled my mother's dream of having a girl after three boys, something she had put off after my brother Ritchie was born. I guess because she was fearful of any problems and not having a healthy a baby. But there she was, beautiful little MaryAnn. You know we doted over her.

One day, Buzzy, Steven and I were down in my basement singing "I Get Around," by The Beach Boys. We were so impressed with ourselves that we decided we would form a group. We called ourselves, "The Classics," even though we already knew that was the name of a famous group. We liked the name and we figured this was just for fun and maybe some local parties. We sort of practiced on and off that year. The thing that excited me now was dad talking about buying one of those brand new portable hi-fi sets that were being advertised. But we had to wait. Dad was taking vacation, and we'd see after vacation. That was the explanation Mom told us, and we accepted it without question.

It was a good vacation. We went to Palisades Amusement Park in New Jersey.

We got to see DJ Cousin Brucie and his show. We went out to Jones Beach and the aqua show at night. Last but not least we all got dressed up for our annual treat at the Chinese Restaurant around the corner. My father knew the owner, and he always had to tell us the story of his success, of how he started out under the "el" (elevated subway) shining shoes and had saved enough money to open the restaurant. By the end of vacation week, we headed to Floyd Bennett stores down Flatbush Avenue. Surprise, surprise! Mom and Dad were picking out that hi-fi they had promised. They told me to pick out records to take home.

I was so excited. There were aisles with bins full of records. I almost didn't know where to begin. I knew that I was going to pass on 45s and get some albums for a change. Now besides listening to my transistor radio while I lie in bed every night, I had a great sounding hi-fi to listen to—all the great songs I loved during the day.

Then tragedy struck. I was in school when the nuns brought us down to pray.

President Kennedy had been shot. I felt a lump in my chest. I think everybody took it personally, because everyone seemed to love him. I don't remember at what point we found out that the president had died. It was almost as if we died. For weeks we watched all the stunning images on TV. I watched traumatized by the funeral procession through Washington. How would we ever go on?

Go on we did. The world as we knew it was starting to change. With January brought a new focus on life. The Beatles were coming, a group that would influence modern music perhaps more than any of its generation.

We inherited a new president who would pass more legislation, especially for human rights and equality, than any other president. President Johnson would not only awaken the hopes and dreams of many Americans but also lead the country down a road of division and despair with the ever-consuming Vietnam War. Was the country ready for any of this? I don't think so, but we continued to go forward.

With the introduction of the Beatles and all the groups that were to follow, it sparked my friends Buzzy, Steven and me to become more serious with our little group in the same way years before Elvis had sparked everyone's interest in rock and roll. We started to practice on a regular basis. We would do this every week without fail and whenever we could squeeze time in between. We played some backyard parties but mostly entertained ourselves.

Life went on routinely for a few years. We were absorbed with school, sports, and girls, but not necessarily in that order. We went to a lot of record hops at the church. They were usually hosted by WMCA "good guys." We got to hear a lot of great music and dance to some very good local groups and some great star acts.

My father had no problem letting me go to the dances because he loved listening to WMCA. First thing when he got up for work in the morning the radio went on. He'd be dancing around the kitchen to Joe O'Brien and Benny in the morning show. We woke up to rock and roll every morning.

You know I have to back up a minute. I talk about living routinely back then, but what we considered routine is not routine today. Amidst all the school, fun and play we were all working already. As I was graduating from junior high, I asked my mother if I could have $2 to go out with my friends. I got the third degree. "What do you need $2 for? You know you're going into high school. You're going to want new clothes and things. You can't be asking for money all the time. You'd better start looking for a job. You give me your salary; I'll give you an allowance out of it and save the rest in the bank for you."

It sounded good to me. I roamed up and down the Avenue in and out of every store, until I landed a job in a toy and paper warehouse on Avenue U. I applied for working papers and took the job at 13 years of age. By 1965, my first year in high school, I was taking home $28 a week. I gave my mother $25 and kept $3 for myself. That was a lot of money for me back then. If you wanted to get drunk with your friends on a street corner you could buy a quart of beer for .20 to .25 cents.

In the meantime Dad was getting ready to open his own transmission shop.

Taking on a partner named Benny, they opened Imperial Transmissions in January 1966. I was still working in the warehouse after school, so I would work in the shop on weekends.

Once school was over I quit the warehouse and went to work for my dad. I learned the transmission business and auto repair. I liked working on cars so I continued working for my father. I took to mechanics very well. Unfortunately school and I were not getting along. It got so bad that I told my father I wanted to quit high school and work full time. His words of wisdom convinced me I should tough it out. I guess I was going through the usual teenage phases.

My friends and I were still into mischief: Shooting pool, drinking beer, listening to records, and still having brawls with other street gangs. Most of the fights seemed to have been over girls, especially with the older guys, but we all stood by each other no matter what.

Growing up is a learning experience, as it is through life. With each episode that you encounter, you also learn about yourself. Many times you don't realize what you are made of until you contemplate retrospectively. It might take many, years later for self-understanding. Sometimes we're in a hurry to grow up, only to find out we can't handle it responsibly.

It's a beautiful spring day and our friend Harry finds out both his folks and older brother and sister are going to be gone from the house a few days. That means he'd have the house all to himself. All that wonderful responsibility eluded Harry; he was able to talk another five of us into playing hooky and using the house as a booze parlor. One hundred-proof Southern Comfort was the order of the day, with some beer chaser to boot.

Buzzy, Steven, Cos and Harry were drinking the hard stuff.

Robert and I had never drunk hard liquor before, so we stayed away from it.

After some hard drinking our four older buddies were polluted. Robert and I were lit so I was smart enough to stop after a few beers. Robert kept going. It wasn't but a short time after that Harry's home became Harry's vomit house. The guys were so bad they couldn't all make the sinks or bathrooms in the house. Somehow, I became everyone's nursemaid and custodian. I ran around crazily with a couple of basins, one in each hand, holding heads up to keep them from drowning themselves.

What a mess! I had more respect and felt more responsible for Harry's house than he did. Plus I had to make sure we didn't get caught. After all, we were supposed to be in school. Once these geniuses recouped a little, they decided to go sit out on the stoop. I was against this and tried to convince them not to. But I couldn't control them.

They were still drunk.

Oh no! Here came one of the neighbors, Mrs. Schirippa. She was from Argentina and didn't speak any English. The guys are trying to be cool. Buzzy decided to stand up to say hello. He fell over and passed out on the steps. I had all to do to get everybody back in the house. Of course, Mrs. Schirippa followed. She was very concerned and didn't know what was wrong. I struggled to explain to her in Italian that they had been drinking. I also begged her not to tell any of the parents, and I would make sure they learned their lesson. I hoped my being honest would be the key. It seemed to work.

Another monumental moment in a guy's life--I was going on my first date. I asked a girl named Cathy out. She had just moved into the neighborhood. She was very cute, but she needed to get her parents' approval. Evidently it was her first date also. I went to pick her up at 8 O'clock one Saturday evening. Cathy told me her father wanted to talk to me. He gave me strict orders. He wanted her back in by 9:30. Wow, how pressing was that! He said when we got back I could sit and talk with her awhile in the parlor.

We needed to take the bus down Avenue U to transfer to Nostrand Avenue and go south. I figured we'd go to Jahn's Ice Cream Parlor. It would be the only thing we could do in so short a time. I was so stressed out in the restaurant, wishing that the waitress would hurry it up. I kept watching my wristwatch and not really enjoying our time together. I did get her home on time. When we got in the door her dad said we could sit and talk till 10 0'clock then I'd have to go. God, I was so glad when it was over. We saw each other for a short while after that but we really never hit it off, and that was my fault. I was still naive when it came to girls, even at 16. I really was awkward at kissing, so she wasn't too impressed with me. Believe it or not she eventually married this guy Harry that was part of our crowd.

One day we were hanging out in front of the house next door. There was a huge old oak tree, and we used to congregate under it. Years before, the ground was all dirt. It was our favorite spot for shooting marbles. All these years later, it was still our place to gather.

We spotted our friend Harry from up the block. He was dressed in a way we never saw him before--bell bottoms and sandals, flowered shirt, beads around his neck and bandana around his head. This guy Charlie turns to him and says, "What the fuck are you supposed to be!?" We all cracked up.

Harry defiantly said, "I like it. I think I look very groovy."

"Groovy, what kind of hippie shit is that?" another person asked. We made fun of Harry the rest of the day.

The crowd was starting to change. I had a very difficult time handling this. The guys I grew up with and loved, the friends that I thought would be friends forever, were changing. They were starting to experiment with drugs, and the music was changing. It wasn't all of us, though. A number of us separated ourselves from the rest, and we did less and less hanging out together.

For some reason we started to drift back more into the culture of our youth. For us it became the 1950s all over again. We were comfortable there. It was where we belonged. It was good times, simple and far away from the people and the world that was taking shape in front of us. This became our rebellion. We were rebelling. We wanted our world to stay the same. We were happy in it. We took our frustrations out on other street gangs. We had numerous fights.

One that I can recall was when a gang of guys came down the block as we were hanging out in front of a three story apartment complex. There were about a dozen of them with their heads buried in glue bags as they walked passed us. It was almost as if they were doing it on purpose, testing us. There were about seven or eight of us. Magoo, Carl and I glanced at each other as the rest of our guys waited for our response.

What balls! How could they walk down our turf in front of our faces and do this? We nodded a silent "Let's go" to each other as they passed. The moment we got off the stoop they took flight. We chased them, catching them on Avenue V as they turned the corner and stood their ground. We slapped the shit out of them as we went by. Carl and I chased the last one down under the "el" at 15th street. Carl rapped the guy over the head with a 2x3 as we sang "Goodnight My Love" by Jesse Belvin. I knew at that point that we were becoming sickos, but that's what kept our turf clean in a neighborhood that was turning to drugs.

The following weeks brought more havoc. I was down in my basement at home when voices yelled in my alleyway, "Bobby, Bobby, hurry, they got your brother, and they got zips!"

As I ran up the outside cellar steps I pulled my garrison belt off my pants, wrapped it around my fist and ran up the block with the guys that called me. In the front yard between two houses stood my brother Stevie with a zip gun under his chin surrounded by about 10 other guys from this gang. They were also holding some of my guys at bay because they were outnumbered and were afraid for my brother.

My friend Robert made an advance toward these guys just as I arrived. Another one of them pulled a BB gun and shoved it into his throat. I didn't know what their beef was and I didn't care. I turned quickly and decked the biggest guy who seemed to be in charge. With this all hell broke loose. I heard my guys yelling "rumble!"

I was on top of the guy beating the hell out of him when I'd started to hear screams. A woman screamed, "Stop! You're killing him." It was Mrs. Gambino, Robert's mother, who lived two doors down. I felt arms around me pulling me off. I couldn't reach this guy to swing any more so I clawed my fingers into his face and eyes. It was adults pulling me off. With this the gang took off. I don't recall now if we ever knew what it was about.

I continued to struggle to get out of high school. As I spent time in detention every day, the teacher in charge took a liking to me. She said with some effort on my part she could set me up in a course that was brand new and just about to begin. It was called the co-op course in which you went to school one week and then worked the next week. This would help get me out of high school, since I hated school so much. The key was to maintain grades and do well on the job that they would set up for me. What more could I ask for?

My whole attitude changed. I did great in school that year. I was tops in many of my classes. I did my best to be the best I could be. That was the promise I made to the teacher that did this for me. I loved the job. I went to work in the print shop of New York City Planning Commission in Manhattan right across the street from the Municipal Building and a block away from City Hall.

There were three others that were given jobs at City Planning also on the co-op course. One fellow named Gary came with me from Brooklyn. He was a train buff and wore a hat like Murray the K except with a feather in it. Gary was into being classy and having, in his words, "finesse."

There were two other students from Queens, NY, by the names of Mike and Jimmy who looked like they were both straight out of 1956. Jimmy, I had no use for. He was a nice guy but a glue head. According to him he always had a cold. Duh! Mike on the other hand was just like me. He seemed to have been brought up the same and had the same attitude about life as I did. We shared many views and had much in common. Mike told me he was originally from Flatbush and Flatlands Avenue; then his family moved to Flushing, Queens.

Mike and I were a great team at work. Our supervisor Louie would give us two to three days of work that sometimes Mike and I would finish in a half day. We were very organized and always worked with a system. The only problem was this idle time led us to do things that we shouldn't have. We were interested in making money so we printed up documents that we felt people would pay to have. But we soon stopped when we saw headlines in the Daily News that "City Planning Commission" was to come under investigation.

As I worked across from Mike at a desk we shared I was singing to myself. Mike was singing to himself. As we overheard each other, Mike looked up with a startled "oh no! You like oldies?"

"Yea, I do. You too?" I asked, smiling.

"Oh my God, I can't believe this—nobody knows all the old songs anymore!" Mike exclaimed.

We started to reminisce about the old days, the days we grew up in. We realized we had more in common than we imagined. We became great friends, true friends, still to this day, that I tell this story forty years later. We were actually excited to have found each other. We spent the rest of that work year hunting for old records on our lunch hour in lower Manhattan. Sometimes in between we would walk down to the site of the new construction for the Twin Towers that were going up and watched in amazement.

Mike invited me to his house in Flushing one Saturday. I had never traveled that far from home on the subway. For me this was going to be an adventure. Three train changes and a hope and prayer not to get lost. I left early in the morning and arrived there about 11:00 am. His house was across the street from Flushing Cemetery, which seemed very creepy to me.

When I got to the door I was greeted by Mike and a large German shepherd named Mr. Fugua, named after Harvey Fugua, lead singer of the Moonglows.

"Get that damn dog in here," I heard Mike's mother yell as she came from behind and grabbed Mr. Fugua's collar. The dog was barking, but I couldn't tell if he wanted to play or eat me. "That's my mom," Mike introduced.

"Hi, I'm Bobby."

"Hi, Bobby. Why don't you boys go down the basement while I tie up the dog and prepare something for lunch?"

As I ventured down the steps, I heard music. It was Mike's brother, Stevie, singing and playing the guitar. Being with them that day was like a blast from the past. I hadn't sung in quite a few years since my group The Classics faded away. Hitting harmonies again with Mike and Stevie sent goose bumps up my spine. Stevie and I took turns on the guitar, too.

"Wow! Bobby really has that old sound. What a blend! We should put something together with Tommy," Stevie said to Mike.

"Who's Tommy?" I asked.

"Tommy's got a great bass voice. He's even sung with the Devotions who did

'Rip Van Winkle.'"

"Sounds great. Put it together," I said.

That spring the four of us got together out in Long Beach. Mike's grandmother had a bungalow there and the family would visit.

Tommy lived in Long Beach so it made it easy for him. I hitched a ride with Magoo, another one of my friends from East 19th Street, and the only one in the crowd with a car. He earned this nickname because of his uncanny resemblance to the cartoon character and his ability for getting into the same awkward situations. As long as you filled a cup on the dashboard of Magoo's Chevy Nova with some change, you got a ride. But Magoo loved the music, too. So he was anxious to go meet on a street corner on Beech Street, in front of a Chinese takeout called "Ping Pong." it was great. What a session. It was the 1950's all over again for us. It was a sound, a blend, a natural for us, the kind of group that you wouldn't have to rehearse a song to death. Everybody blended and knew their spots instinctively. Mike was primary lead. Stevie and I shared first, second and over-tenor positions, while Tommy filled in with bass and baritone.

"APOSTLES"
Left to Right: Mike Knox, Tom Martino, Stevie Knox, Bobby Monti (Center)

Mike would get so excited sometimes when we got together that he would go blank. By that I mean he would lose track of where he was and what he was doing. Mike would say we're like the apostles of rock 'n roll as crowds would gather around to listen. We soon adopted the name Apostles for our group. Sometimes other vocal groups would come to the corner to let us hear them. It was like a battle of the groups. And when they'd hear us, they'd say "Wow, you guys are great! We'll be back." They knew they couldn't compete. It made us feel really good.

School was finally coming to a close. Everyone was ready for graduation and making plans for the future. Mike and Gary were staying on at City Planning, and I was going full time at my father's shop. Graduation day was a farce and a disgrace in some ways. The ceremony took place in Loews Theater on Flatbush Avenue. It was a beautiful place, but it was full of rhetoric and anti-Americanism in speeches from all the radical hippies that took to the podium. My friends and I that graduated ignored it all and passed a bottle of Southern Comfort back and forth between us. I was so glad to be finished with school, but also proud of myself for getting through it.

I continued singing with the guys in my crowd back in Brooklyn with Joey D, Savage and myself on the corner of E. 19th street and Avenue U. That's what we did when we weren't shooting pool or at a record party that the girls were having.

Later I got a phone call from Mike. He was talking to Gary and they wanted to get together one evening on E. 19 St. to hang out and have some fun. Mike would come with some of his other friends that he wanted me to meet, and Gary would come with his friends. Gary lived about six blocks from me and cruised onto E. 19 Street on Saturday night in a '64 Lincoln with suicide doors. Out popped Albert with his two brothers. I already knew them. Sometimes they hung out with us. Their family owned an Italian bakery on Avenue U and E. 12^{0}' Street.

Albert was just about the biggest used hubcap dealer in the neighborhood.

A '55 Chevy pulled up with a guy named Johnny driving. Mike in front and this other guy Dave who looked like a short Elvis, along with Mike's brother Stevie who we used to call "Satch" in the back seat. We started to hang out in front of my house for a while, hitting notes like always. Albert started to tell us that some guys on Kings

Highway were harassing Gary before they came here, because he looked funny to them. Gary stepped forward from behind the four of us singing. He was very thin. You might even say scrawny, but a nice guy. With his deep voice he said, "Maybe we should pay them a little visit." Gary had such a great deep voice; too bad he couldn't sing.

We all agreed with his request and started walking towards Kings Highway, singing as we walked the streets. We figured if these bullies had a problem with Gary who looked like Mr. Debonair, they would surely have a problem with us. We'd just have to straighten that out. We looked like the East Side Kids 50's style. Black leather vest, sleeveless T-shirts, garrison belts to the side, motorcycle boots, greased back DA haircuts. Some of us sported fedoras and baseball caps with the rims flipped up. I had a fedora on with a small brass star pinning the brim back like "Chiefie" of the Bowery Boys

When we got to the Highway, some of us went into a small candy store for Cokes, The rest of us hung outside and waited. Kings Highway was always a very busy area with lots of people shopping. Sure enough as I waited, out of the crowd a few guys approached me. One of them walked right up to my face and said, "You look like a yoyo!" and I responded pissed off, "and you're going to look like a yo-yo when I bounce you from here to the moon and back!" One of his buddies said, "Be cool, be cool," as a couple of cops were approaching us.

"All right boys, let's break it up." There were too many of us congregating in one place. One cop asked me "Do you boys live around here."

"No," I responded.

"Then I suggest you make your way back where you come from."

I turned to everyone. "Let's go."

We started to walk south down East 1 8th street. As we got about three quarters of the way down the block, Carl noticed that we were being followed by a gang. We stood our ground. I asked Gary if these were the ones that had bothered him, and he told me they were. As they got closer they started running towards us. I knew what was coming. The same guy that had commented to me on the highway headed straight for me. I didn't want to take the first shot, so I hit him hard enough to floor him.

"Come on, tough guy, get up!" I stood over him and waited. He charged into me with what became a wrestling match. As we scuffled,

Carl and my boys set a perimeter circling us. His people stepped back. I heard Carl and Savage yelling, "One on one, one on one," holding their ground.

There was no way he was going to beat me. I had taken many a beating over the years, and I promised myself that I would never take a beating again. I had wrestled with my brother all my life just about every day, and I also won my division in high school wrestling my junior year.

We were wrestling in between parked cars out in the street. I had him in headlock he couldn't get out of. As I was squeezing his head, a couple of cars crept by with flowers painted on them and long-haired hippies hanging out of the windows, screaming, "peace, brothers!"

"Fuck you!" was our unison response. The two cars hurried off realizing they were in the wrong place at the wrong time. My buddy still couldn't get out of the headlock I had him in. Out of desperation and not being able to breathe, he sunk his teeth into my side. I yelled out "son of a bitch!" I grabbed his hand and bit into it like a true Italian would. With that we heard yells of "cops, oops!" As sirens started to blare in the distance we all broke up. We ran a block and then decided to be cool. There were too many of us walking together so we decided to split up into smaller groups as we made our way back to Avenue U.

Suddenly two squad cars pulled up. We didn't run. We were very cool. Cops lined us up against their cars and patted us down. They singled out Albert's brother Louie. He was bigger than the rest of us, so they figured he was the leader. "Where are you guys from?"

Louie answered "Avenue U."

"Avenue U and where?" pressed the cop.

"East 19th Street." One cop said, "It figures."

"Look, you boys better get back to Avenue U and behave yourselves the rest of the night; otherwise we'll teach you what a real beating is!"

When we got back to our turf, E. 19 and Avenue U, we all regrouped inside Trio Pizza Parlor. (Hands down, it was the best pizza in Brooklyn at that time.) Mike was making a few phone calls in case we needed some help. I told him squash that. I didn't think it would be necessary. Everybody discussing it felt it was over. Out of the pizza place Gary and his friends went home. We walked back to the front of my house to hang out again.

Suddenly Johnny, who had driven down from Flushing, said, "Uh, we gotta go." He jumped into his car hurriedly. Stevie, Dave, and Mike said quick goodbyes.

Mike glanced at me and said, "Oh shit, Bobby, are your guys be all right? I am sorry--Johnny's never seen anything like this. He is in a panic"

Mike and I both looked up the block. There were about thirty guys coming toward us. I told Mike, "Don't worry, we'll be all right."

As they pulled away, Mike said, "Call me!" There were seven of us left. I didn't sweat anything. The guys from the block, the E. 19 Street Boys, were used to this. We were always outnumbered in any fights we were ever in. But what was about to happen we never expected. We all looked at each other with a get ready look.

We heard screeching from the turn onto 19th Street. As we looked, another thirty plus bodies piled out of cars and were coming toward us from Avenue V. We were surrounded. There was a sort of calmness as we glanced at each other. We knew there was nowhere to go. We were going to fight like never before. With that, four screeching cars stopped right in front of us. Unloading their bully partners, the guy I fought on Kings Highway charged toward me and tackled me, lifting me onto a fender of a car. I started punching him as I went down. All hell broke loose as the sounds of violence were all around us.

Next thing I know, I'm on my back with this guy on top. I'm holding him at arm's length with my left hand and punching him in the face with the right from the ground up. All of a sudden my brother Stevie is pulling back on the guy's head as I'm hitting him.

Out of the commotion I saw my father grabbing this guy yelling "get off him!"

My father throws him off into the car parked at the curb. As I jump up from the sidewalk I see my mother at the door with my little sister MaryAnn who was begging, "I want to see the action!" and my mother yelling at her to get in the house. Once up from the ground I see all my guys swinging away with fists, belts, broomstick handles. I couldn't believe all the men that came out of their houses to help us. I saw Mr. Pampinella holding back two guys and my friend going at it with a guy next to him screaming, "I'll take you all on!" What an asshole.

Once again the cops raced down East 19 Street heading the wrong way from the one way street from Avenue U and from Avenue V and on foot. As lights and sirens blared, the cops broke everything up as they rounded everybody up. You wouldn't believe how many people they had assuming the position on their cars and on the patrol cars. As they were getting patted down the cops were going through their vehicles bringing out bottles and bottles of liquor and emptying them right in the street.

The 19th Street seven stood on the sidewalk. We all couldn't help but have smirks on our faces. To have come out of this unscathed was a miracle. We grimaced to each other as we watched the police empty Southern Comfort bottles, the official drink of E 19 Street!

I called Mike the next day. I caught a lot of flax from my E. 19th Street Boys for him and his friends leaving. He apologized and said, "I knew you'd be okay."

TIME TO GROW UP

It was the summer of 1969. The Vietnam War was raging, and the draft was in effect. You could be called to serve up until the age of 26. I had the ingenious idea of enlisting and getting it over with so I could go on with my life. My friend Robert decided he liked the idea and wanted to do it with me. We went down to the Navy recruiting station in Coney Island and signed up. I went with the Navy because I just thought it would be nice to follow in my father's footsteps. Dad served in 1944 and 1945 and was all set in the Pacific for the invasion of Japan. Now it was my turn. Robert and I went in on the buddy system, which meant we would go through boot camp together in the same company.

Nothing ever goes according to plan. Right before we were to leave for boot camp, we reported to Fort Hamilton. We stood at attention for a physical inspection. They found that I had patches of hair loss behind my head a little above my neck, called alopecia. This held me back another week before my departure. It was just a case of nerves. Once they realized I was safe, I got shipped out, but without Robert.

Boot camp was an experience. My father always said, "Join the service. It'll make a man out of you." I was no stranger to discipline, so I had no problem. They weren't just trying to toughen you up, but weeding out the weak was the mission. It got to a point in boot camp that I actually enjoyed it, even though it was hard being away from home and those you loved.

I saw many a man break, some the most unlikely. Sad, but when you think about it, your life depends on the man next to you and his life on yours. We became a color company that had a great sense of accomplishment. Each company earned flags in competition with other companies on base. We had a chief that was a very determined and driven man. He made us into men he could be proud of. We learned how to be proud, too.

After boot camp we went home for a very brief period awaiting orders for where we'd be deployed. Before I got out of camp we took a lot of placement tests. We filled out applications for positions we thought we would like. At my mother's suggestion, I applied for something in aviation. She thought it would be a good lead into an airport job after my military service. I hoped it wouldn't go the way of my mother's high school suggestion--to take an academic course that would lead to college along with the hardest high school French classes which would also be good for college.

While waiting for orders to move on, I got a phone call from this fellow Mike who was a boot camp buddy. He was making arrangements with two other sailors for a weekend reunion of sorts. Mike and Bruce, both from Long Island, would pick me up in Brooklyn and then take a ride up to Connecticut to visit this other friend Scotty who had a nice piece of property and home. Scotty would make arrangements for us to meet girls Saturday evening. His uncle left him use of his log cabin. We could have a great night. Scotty said to bring our dress blues because the girls were anxious to meet some sailors and they'd be very impressed by us.

Mike and Bruce picked me up with Mike's '64 Impala, and we cruised up to Connecticut. It was a nice ride. I remember Mike flipping out when Peggy Sue by Buddy Holly was playing on the radio. He started pumping the gas pedal saying how it was his favorite song. We had some fun on our way there. Scotty greeted us when we arrived and started showing us around. It seemed to me, a city boy that his cabin was located in quite a remote area, but it was very beautiful. He did have some property—a lot of acreage.

We spent the afternoon shooting out windows of late 40's automobiles that were on different parts of the property. Scotty had a number of different rifles and shotguns. We all took turns shooting. I guess this is what you do for excitement when you live in the sticks!

The night sky sparkled with stars as I stepped out of the Impala in front of Scotty's cabin. I couldn't help but notice how full of light the sky was on this crisp February night as Scotty fumbled for the right key to open the door. As we walked in, Scotty found the lights. You could tell no one had used the cabin in some time. It was kind of musty and cold, like walking into a pocket of cold air. The place was really nice though, with rustic themed decorations. We brought beer and bags of chips in.

We knew we had better warm up the place before the girls got there. On the right side of the cabin almost in line with the door entrance there was a fireplace in the center of the living room wall. Mike and Bruce started to work on getting a fire started. Scotty and I tried to make the place livable and cozy looking. Some time went by, and the boys were still struggling with the fireplace. A knock on the door said the girls were here. Scotty opened the door and in walked four beautiful girls. Scotty introduced everyone. They were impressed with us in our dress blue Navy uniforms. We knew this was going to be a great little party.

The girls were cold so Mike reassured them he'd have a fire going in a few minutes. I said to Mike and Bruce, "You guys have tried everything—you haven't got the fire going yet?"

Bruce said, "Bobby, you're from Brooklyn. You should know how to start a fire."

"Yeah, well, maybe you should get a few drops of gas and throw it on," I joked.

Mike jumped up from squatting over the logs. "All right, why didn't I think of that?"

"Mike, are you serious? I was only kidding!" I said.

"No, no, that's a good idea," he insisted.

Mike went out the door to siphon some gas out of the Impala. I couldn't believe he was really going to do that. I was very concerned as was Scotty. Bruce promised, "Don't worry, we'll be careful."

Mike came back in with a full eight ounce plastic cup of gas and handed it to Bruce. "That's too much!" Scotty shouted.

Bruce started to drizzle the gasoline over the logs. From a fire place that looked cold and dead there must have been something smoldering. In a flash the fireplace exploded! The flames burst from the fireplace like a bomb. A flame traveled up the drizzle to the cup. In an instant Bruce panicked and his instinct was to get rid of the cup. He turned and threw the cup behind him, not realizing I was standing there. In a heartbeat I was engulfed in flames. I was soaked in gas from my shoulders and chest down to the front of my shins. My body was a ball of fire.

I didn't hear the girls screaming or the guys yelling. All I could hear were my own thoughts. Something was telling me to stay calm as I tried to pat myself out. Mike was beside me trying to put me out also. It seemed like the more I patted myself the more engulfed I became. Oh shit! Fuck! Oh Fuck, fuck, fuck! I was starting to panic as I cursed. I glanced over at the girls who were cringing at the sight of me, feeling almost embarrassed at my language and not caring all at the same time.

Even though I was starting to panic I was still thinking. I glanced around the cabin and realized there was a carpet underneath the heavy oak dining room set next to the kitchen. I knew somehow I had to get at it in order to wrap myself in it. I ran over to it, hoping that God would give me the strength to pull it out in one shot. I had no time to move furniture. With one quick pull, wrestling with its large size, I watched as everything flew off the table and chairs went flying. But I got it out from under. My mind was telling me I saved myself as I rolled it around me and dropped to the floor, wrapping myself in the heaviness of the carpet. Smoke escaped from in between the layers of carpet. I lay there catching my breath as the guys huddled over me.

"He's ok! He's ok! Bobby, are you all right?" Their voices rang out above me.

They started to un-wrap me. As they opened up the carpet, I burst into flames again. "Oh shit!" the guys covered me up again, the three of them hugging the carpet around me. They let me lay there awhile until they were sure I wouldn't light up again.

They helped me to my feet. The first thing I needed to do was get out of my gas soaked uniform. All of us wanted to call it a night. As we were walking out the door, Scotty told us not to worry about the place. He'd take care of it tomorrow. I didn't realize the damage to the cabin until we were about to leave. The entire wall by the fireplace was charred. Scotty had put it out with an extinguisher.

"My God! We almost burnt the place down!" I said, looking at the damage.

"Never mind that! You're lucky to be walking out alive," Bruce told me with an apology.

I was lucky. I had only reddened skin and the loss of hair over my body.

Someone was watching over me! My dress blues saved my life. When I got home I told everyone I had a good time and never mentioned the incident in Connecticut.

My orders finally arrived in the mail. I was to report to a base in Memphis. I went to Patuxent River, Maryland, a naval air station, for a course in hydraulics. But this wasn't really what I wanted—more schooling. My dislike for school remained strong and here I was, back in the thick of it again.

I tried to make the best of it. What I really wanted was to be a sailor on a ship. It didn't look like that was going to happen any time soon. I shuttled back and forth from Maryland to Brooklyn a number of weekends until my schooling was through. Now I waited for orders again.

My papers arrived, and I was going overseas to Naval Air Station, Guam. I was to be stationed for eighteen months there and then finish my military service at sea on an aircraft carrier.

As I first arrived on Guam I was amazed at how hot and humid it was. I marveled at the beauty of the island as I journeyed to the air base. It was ironic to think about its beauty at this point in time knowing the horrors of battle that went on there during World War II

I reported to my squadron only to find out that I was going to be working in the galley on kitchen duty for the next three months. I was disheartened that I wouldn't be working on these great looking aircraft that were in the hangers. The aircraft I would be working on eventually was used for observing weather conditions. I found out later from guys in my barracks that the plane was used for observing a lot of things besides weather. Everyone at one time or another would be making trips to Vietnam. I never wrote home about this because I didn't want my family worrying.

I became friends with a few guys, and we hung out together in our off-duty hours. There wasn't much to do in our off time. There was only one TV station on the island. I found it funny that dozens of guys would crowd into the air conditioned recreation rooms to watch nothing but soap operas all day. It was surprising to realize how many of them got hooked on these shows.

The USO club was a cool place to go and have a few drinks. Sometimes they would have girls dancing burlesque. That always drew cheers from sailors and marines alike. On weekends they would have stage shows with all types of performers. I got to see the Four Coins. They were an old vocal group and just my cup of tea. They sang their big hit "Shangri La." Hearing them sing almost made life on Guam worthwhile.

As time went by a fellow sailor that I had befriended by the name of Gary and I decided to chip in to buy a car. Since life on base was so drab, this would allow us some freedom in getting around and to visit different towns on the island. Plus it would be great access to get to a beach. I didn't have a license yet. Gary said he'd teach me how to drive. I had a little knowledge from moving cars around in my dad's shop. I thought it wouldn't take much for me to really drive.

We chipped in and bought a '61 Studebaker, military green, originally used on base by the Navy.

It only needed some minor transmission work, which I had no problem taking care of.

When Gary couldn't take me out for driving lessons, I would wait until late in the evening when the base was quiet from regular activity and the roads on the island were virtually empty. Then I would take the car out on my own to get a better feel of the road and handling of the car. I thought I was doing pretty well and was looking forward to my driving test and my nineteenth birthday that was coming up in October.

One morning as I was getting cleaned up and shaven, I noticed something on the floor in the stall behind me in the mirror. I turned to look with half my face full of shaving cream. It was a wallet, the fattest wallet I'd ever seen! it must have fallen out of someone's pants as they were sitting on the toilet. I didn't look through it. I just picked it up and stuffed it into my slacks. I finished shaving and headed back to my bunk.

There I took it out and started to go through it.

Gary was opening his locker and noticed me. "Whatcha got there?" he asked. With a whisper I said, "You wouldn't believe what I just found in the bathroom." There was a lot of personal and military ID and pictures plus $300 in cash.

Gary said "You're going to split that with your friend, right? Otherwise I'll have to let people know you found this wallet."

Like an idiot I got scared at the sound of that and split the money with him. "Now what do I do with the rest of it? Should I give it back to the guy without the money?" I asked Gary.

Gary looked at me, exasperated, "Are you nuts?" Then he insisted we go for a ride

We took a drive in the car through some of the most desolate roads we knew of. As Gary was driving he said to me, "All right, now empty out the wallet and fling the stuff out the window into the jungle. After everything is gone, toss the wallet."

I was a nervous wreck. I never did anything so dishonest before. Gary seemed to be very cool with it. I was starting to get the impression from him that down deep he wasn't a good person.

My thoughts were confirmed when two weeks later he approached me in the galley while I was working. "I think you should sign over your half of the car to me." "Why should I do that?" I asked.

"I found out who the wallet belonged to, and I might have to let him know you're the one who found it."

"Are you kidding?" I asked, "You're going to blackmail me! I thought you were my friend. I fixed the car for nothing. I gave you half the money. Now you're going to do this to me? Some friend! You know you and I are finished. If I go down, I take you with me. It's my word against yours! "

"All right, all right!" Gary exclaimed. "Forget I said anything. I am your friend. Your birthday is coming up in a few days. We'll go for a ride, and I'll buy the beer and we'll celebrate all night."

Two days later Gary and another friend James approached me in the barracks. "What time do you want us to pick you up tomorrow?" Gary asked.

"James," I said, "You're going to celebrate my birthday, too."

"Hey," Gary said, "He's going to buy the beer, and we've got a great night planned. We'll go into town, meet some nice girls and have a good time."

"Sounds good to me, but I'm on duty until 6 pm. I'll need some time to clean up," I told them both.

"We're on duty also and need to make some rounds on the island. So we'll leave at 8. We've got all night," James said.

The next day, my birthday, went like any other day. The guys were there to pick me up as planned. We left the base. I was in the back seat as Gary drove and James was up in front in the passenger seat. We were all looking forward to an exciting evening. I was relieved I would be off duty for a couple of days.

We stopped at the first small town along the empty roads that led around the island. Gary handed James money to buy beer. We sat in the parking area of a small store for a while as we downed a beer each. Then we were on our way again. The roads were very seldom traveled and were pitch black as we traveled through the jungles. The use of coral was incorporated into the roads and sidewalks creating a slippery surface even when not wet. I continued to drink as Gary drove. I was so tired I eventually passed out lying down on the back seat.

I awoke as I sensed a real increase in speed. I lifted my head and my upper body as I held myself up between the front and back seat. I realized that we were going down a steep hill, when a glare of headlights loomed into the car from a passing vehicle. Gary blurted out, "Oh shit!"

At the bottom of the hill was a 90 degree turn, because a mountain sat dead in front. Gary lost control and flipped the Studebaker as it hurled into the mountain. It bounced and flipped overturning across the road tossing the vehicle into water. I was knocked out on first impact. I didn't remember anything after Gary's first reaction.

When I eventually opened my eyes, we were in shallow water but sinking.

Suddenly flashing lights and rescue workers yelled. I could feel the car being wrenched out of the water. It was a miracle that some other vehicle had just passed us when this happened. They evidently went up ahead for help. If not, I wouldn't be here today.

It wasn't until the car was back on the road did the severity of the crash hit me. I didn't see Gary or James. I was in excruciating pain. My right elbow was at my shoulder; my left leg was behind me, and I was wedged in on the floor between the seats. I couldn't move my left arm. Blood was pouring out of my right knee. I was wet with blood and covered with green paint. There was a gallon can of green paint behind the rear seat that evidently exploded open as the vehicle overturned. The smell of green oil paint and blood was nauseating.

Voices kept reassuring me they would get me out in between my moans of anguish. They were having difficulty because of the way my limbs were positioned. They had to remove the left rear door to get me free of the vehicle. They quickly placed me on the stretcher and into the ambulance. As soon as I was in, the doors closed and we took off, sirens blaring. The EMTs started slicing my pants legs open from the bottom up to my thigh. As they spread the wet blood-soaked material apart, spurs of blood were shooting out of my knee. They concentrated on stopping the bleeding as I lost consciousness.

I opened my eyes as I was being wheeled speedily down a hallway. The EMT told me,

"Don't worry, buddy. We're here." We entered a brightly lit room filled with nurses and doctors. I knew I was in the emergency room of a hospital. I begged them, in my anguish to give me something for pain,

"In a minute, we just need you to answer some quick questions," was the response from a nurse I told them whatever I could. As I glanced away from them looking down the length of the gurney, a priest was draping his holy cloth around his neck and making the sign of the cross. He was preparing to give me last rights. I got scared and started to pray with him as he anointed me with holy oils. Not knowing the extent of my injuries, I thought I was going to die!..I felt a needle pierce my left arm.

I awoke a couple of days later yelling out asking for something for pain so excruciating, I could barely breathe. The bed I lay in was set on an incline from the foot of the bed. My left leg was in traction; my right leg bandaged from my lower thigh to my calf.

My right arm hung above me was also in traction with a long bolt running through my elbow, and I couldn't move my left arm. The medical staff kept shooting morphine into my thighs, and every time they did I'd vomit a short time later. This was the routine all the days ahead consisted of for some time.

A couple of weeks went by until Gary came to visit with his arm in a sling. He asked me how I was. I told him I was hurting. He apologized for the accident. He told me that ironically, he only received a minor injury to his arm. James had gone through the windshield. They removed his spleen and he would need plastic surgery in the future. His face was a mess of scars. He told me that the doctors said they took more time cleaning paint off of us than operating. We both laughed. Gary mentioned the car was totaled and unrecognizable.

I continued to slowly heal, humbled by the whole process. Gradually I realized what was really important in life was to have your health. As I tried to sit on a bed pan as I lay in traction, I believed God was punishing me for the wrong action I had taken with the wallet. My conscience would carry that burden for many years to come.

By the second week of December they took me out of traction. It was an incredible relief to get out of bed and into a wheelchair. My right arm was placed in a cast. I needed to learn to walk again from my hip and knee injuries. The first biggest challenge was to get from the wheelchair to the toilet on my own. These are the trials that make a person learn to appreciate life.

Out of boredom I wheeled in and out of other wards in the naval hospital, just to say hello to guys and see how they were doing. The hospital was full of casualties from Nam. The most traumatizing was going through the amputee ward. The images I witnessed, the pain and anguish of these young men, the lives destroyed, were heartbreaking and embedded in my memory.

My doctors gave me the news that they were sending me home. I was filled with mixed emotions but excited about going home. James visited with me. His face was a mess of torn flesh and scarring, but he was feeling good. We wished each other well. He was returning to duty expecting plastic surgery later. When I saw Gary I asked him if he could pack my belongings and make arrangements for my sea bag to be sent home with me. He wished me luck and said he'd take care of everything. I really didn't trust him, but I had no other choice.

I was medevac'd on the large Air Force transport plane, along with many other injured sailors and marines. We were all on stretchers and placed on racks inside the plane. I was not one of the lucky ones to get a rack. There wasn't enough room for me, so I was secured on the floor.

The flight home was a surprise. I thought we were going to head back toward the states, but instead we flew to Japan then up to Alaska where we disembarked for a three day stay at a hospital there. We took off again to Chicago, then McGuire's Air Force Base in New Jersey. My final transport was a helicopter ride to St. Albans Naval Hospital in Queens, New York. I thought I'd never get home. It was such a great feeling, to be home again in time for Christmas, and an incredible thrill to see mom and dad as tears welled in their eyes. I was just starting to walk again. It was going to be a great Christmas!

I would spend the next six months convalescing at St. Albans and then placed on light duty. I served at the Brooklyn Navy Yard for a while, and then onto Navy special services in the municipal building in lower Manhattan. I eventually received a Navy letter telling me I would be sent back to regular duty. I knew I was not physically capable to perform regular duty.

I went to a number of private doctors who wrote letters and medical reports advising the opposite. I went as far as enlisting the aid of my Congressman and gave him the medical documentation, asking him if he could help in getting me released from active duty. I was very disappointed, because I really had always had my heart set on being on board ship.

Next, a set of orders came and I was on my way to Norfolk, Virginia, to be released from active service. I was getting an honorable medical discharge and placed on the temporary retirement list. I was also going to receive a pension check from the Navy every month.

I would soon realize how important that was going to be.

Upon release from the Navy, I started to look for civilian work. I didn't really want to go back to transmission work. I took a lot of tests and applied for all kinds of city and utility jobs, basically for the benefits the private sector did not offer.

I did well on all written tests and on interviews but never passed the physicals for any of the positions I applied for. So, I fell back on my skills and back to dad's shop doing transmission work. It was not that doing transmission work was physically easy, on the contrary, it was quite demanding. However, working for my father would enable me to work at my own pace. If I needed help with something, it was not a problem, because everyone was aware that I had limitations. I gradually started to make my way to doing more bench work where I wasn't so physically taxed.

PING PONGS

Life started to fall back to a routine as I worked a lot of hours. I hung out with the old crowd singing on the street corners. I was back to singing with the Apostles, and performing at parties again was a great feeling. I had Doo Wop running through my veins. From the way the old crowd carried on you'd swear it was still 1956. Any rock 'n roll show that had the old groups you can bet we were there!

There was a resurgence of the music for quite some time. The shows had all the great disc jockeys of the day hosting them, Murray the K, Norman Knight, Scott Muni and Gus Gossett, to name a few. Jocko Henderson and even Jerry Blavat from Philly would show up occasionally. Sometimes it really felt like we never left the era we grew up in.

I started dating Lizzie who lived up in Flushing, Queens. My friend Mike set me up with her. He had dated her in the past and told me she was a good girl. She was very pretty, and I liked her a lot.

I started doing a lot of driving. I had just recently gotten my license. I bought a '37 Oldsmobile that my father tried to talk me out of. I always had this thing for old cars.

He told me "Son, if you want a car, you'll have to buy it, repair it, insure it, and maintain it. It's yours, and it's your responsibility." Those were Dad's words of wisdom. Back then, nobody got a car because they graduated or achieved anything else other than their own independence. Eventually the Oldsmobile broke down. What bad timing, because they were starting to shoot scenes for the movie "The Godfather" and had solicited my Olds to be in the film. I could not make the necessary repairs to the car to prepare it for the movie. It needed major engine work, so I started to slowly dismantle the car in my folks' driveway.

I still needed transportation, so I picked up a '57 Caddy Coupe De Ville. A pretty car, it was powder blue and white. Of course I jazzed it up. I installed blue crush velvet headliner tufted with clear buttons. Even mom helped. It looked like the night sky when we finished. I also did the dashboard with the same blue velvet material. What a car! She was a rocket ship! I did a lot of cruisin' from

Brooklyn to Long Beach where I'd sing all night with the group outside Ping Pongs, on Beech St., probably one of the first Chinese take outs.

One night as I was cruising down Beech Street my friend Eddie yelled to me as I passed him by. Eddie was a church custodian and a great guy and true greaser. We had been out hustling for a couple of bucks on private sanitation trucks in the evenings, there was an ongoing strike with sanitation, and the private sector was picking up the slack. Eddie and I decided to cash in, Eddie was cool. He had a gold colored '60 Corvair with

"Destiny" written in script across its front fenders, As 1 cruised down Beech Street and stopped at the light, Eddie approached me at the corner, calling my name to get my attention.

"Heyyy, Destiny, what's happening?" I answered him.

"Hey, are you going on the truck with me tonight?" he asked.

"Gee, I don't know Eddie," I said doubtfully.

"Come on Bobby! We will make some good money tonight!" Eddie persisted.

"I don't know Eddie, something's telling me to go home." I turned and looked toward the right of my seat as if someone were sitting there telling me to go home. "Maybe you should skip tonight, too," I suggested. "I'll go with you next time, I promise. [1]

Disappointed, he asked, "Are you sure?"

I assured him I was and told him I'd see him tomorrow.

A few days later, the phone rang, and my mom answered, "Yes, Mike, he's right here, hold on." Handing the phone to me, I said hi to my buddy Mike, "Yeah, Slicker, what's up?" A panicked voice greeted me. "Bobby, are you sitting down? I've got bad news. They just found Eddie's body in Valley Stream!"

Stunned, I said, "What! What happened?"

Mike continued, "It happened the night he went out on the truck without you. Evidently the guy he was with had a contract out on him. They hit him and took Eddie out, too, with two bullets to the back of the head!"

I felt sick, "Oh God! I was supposed to go with him. Something kept telling me to go home. If I went with him, I'd be dead, too! "

"Bobby, your guardian angel was watching over you. It wasn't your time yet" Mike said.

I took it hard. I still miss Eddie, to this day. I fell apart at the funeral parlor. The whole gang from Brooklyn and the Long Beach crowd showed up in their black leather jackets and engineer boots. We knew Eddie would have wanted it that way, and we did it out of respect for him. My girl, Lizzie, refused to go with me for some reason I can't recall, and that upset me on top of everything else. From our earliest days, she had a way of disappointing me.

Now I think back to all the times when Eddie would call me in off the street. He had a house close to the beach. It was a dead-end street. Sometimes we would meet with the crowd before hitting the beach or just hang out there, in front of his house with Eddie's Gold Cowair parked outside his house. We could hear the doo-wops pouring out his front door. He'd call me in, "Bobby! Listen to this", and he'd play some outrageous a cappella doo-wop record by some great group. We'd stand there getting goose bumps on our arms and Eddie would say

"Wow, I can't believe I lived all this!" "We all did, Eddie, my old friend, we all did."

One day while working under the lift servicing a '63 Caddy, I was singing along to on old doo-wop on the radio. The customer standing nearby was watching me work on his vehicle. He heard me singing and remarked "You like that old rock 'n roll?"

"Yeah" I replied. "I have this group I sing with, that's all we do."

"You're kidding! I have a group too, called The Premiers. Ever hear of them?" "Can't say that I have," I said as I reached for a wrench.

The customer continued, "It's basically me, my two brothers and a friend. My name is Michael. We participated in Ted Mack's amateur hour years ago!"

"Really, wow! " I said, pretty impressed. We shook hands, grease and all. Then he told me he also had his own recording studio and would love to hear my group. He told me if he felt we were good he'd record us and we could maybe go from there. I became very excited. The first thing in the door that night I called my friend Mike, our lead singer, and I told him the deal. We made arrangements to get together and audition for this guy Michael at his studio.

We pulled up to the address—a private house in East New York. We couldn't imagine what kind of studio it could be in a private house. We soon found out it was top-of-the-line. There was a bedroom converted into a studio soundproofed and all. There was a glass enclosure with all the recording equipment behind it, a nice board and a number of reel to reel tape machines. Stevie, Tom and I surrounded one microphone and Mike took the lead on a separate mic. We warmed up a little as Michael prepared to record us. Michael's girlfriend Rose was in the studio, also anxious to hear us.

Michael had his back toward us in the booth. I watched him start to spin the tapes on the reels with his fingers helping to get them started. He spoke to us over a speaker, "Whenever you're ready, guys." He was ready to record us. I didn't recall the song we sang. All I knew was that when we were done his eyes lit up and his girl Rose looked shocked. "Wow!" Michael was impressed to say the least when he said, "That was great! You guys are great! Let's talk"

We sat and discussed Michael writing a song for us. We would have input with the lyrics and arrangement. The plan was for Michael to record us and possibly cut a record to promote to the major labels. We met the following week and just about had a song down. "Do You Remember" was the title. It was to be an upbeat doo-wop. I had my reservations about it really making it big. It was 1971 and what my friends and I loved musically was not really the most popular form of music anymore. But, there was at the time a great resurgence of early rock 'n roll, so who knew what could happen.

We met one night a week at the studio for the next few weeks. The first time back we met all the musicians as they were starting to lay down some tracks for an arrangement of the song. The rest of the evening we added our input on the arrangement figuring out background and vocal harmonies and finalizing on lyrics. With all of us working as a team we made quite a bit of progress that evening, and we were all ready to cut some takes the next week.

The Apostles were pretty excited after leaving the studio that night. We discussed the possibilities of where this could go as we made our way home that evening. Tommy had us cracking up as we had dubbed Michael with the nickname "Toupie." Michael Capitain was very meticulous in how he ran the studio. The way he wore his hair earned him the nickname. He was actually bald. He would comb all his hair forward, from the back of his head into a huge pompadour and hair sprayed it, resembling Elvis.

By our next session we pretty much had the song down. The musicians were back the following week and finished laying down the tracks. The song sounded great. Toupie was such a perfectionist that the next couple of weeks we kept redoing takes so often that I was waking up in the middle of the night with the background repeatedly ringing in my ears

At one point Tommy would have us breaking up at the mic. In the middle of doing backup vocals, he had a way of taking his hands and shifting his head in the middle of our singing as if to adjust his toupee, and we would burst out laughing. We finally reached the point where Toupie was satisfied. The finished product sounded great.

Now it was onto side B. This is where the problems began. Toupie wrote a song that the guys just refused to do. We felt it was too juvenile and not with the serious doowop R&B sound that we had. Toupie was steadfast in running the show at that point. The Apostles then decided not to work any further with him. We stayed in touch with Toupie, but went our separate way, continuing to do house parties, street corners and a couple of concerts at Long Beach City Hall, where of course, we got skunked for our money. Our second concert we weren't even happy with ourselves or our performance. People were looking for a later form of music that just wasn't us.

Strangely, one of the guys in the crowd, Jerry, who was a little on the strange side, never told me that my girl Lizzie was his sister. Neither one of them mentioned anything until I pulled up to Lizzie's house in Flushing, Queens. I saw Jerry outside. I said to him, "What are you doing

"I live here, jerk. Lizzie is my sister," he said, somewhat annoyed.

I was flabbergasted, "You're kidding! Now I know why she acts strangely toward me sometimes. What did you tell her? "

"I told her you were crazy, Jocko," Jocko was a nickname Mike gave me that stuck for years.

Lizzie lived in a garden apartment, ratty and rundown. She took care of two brothers and her father, who had poor health due to emphysema. She was the only one working and tried to make the place a home. I was impressed with her for taking on so much. I was never crazy about staying overnight as the place was roach infested. It was the kind of place where the kids peed in the hallways and people threw garbage out of their top floor windows. I did stay on occasion, only because I had fallen asleep at the wheel at 4 AM one Sunday morning on the ride home. Thank God a passerby kept blowing his horn until I woke up.

I was starting to run myself ragged. I stayed up late, worked long hours, drove back and forth through three New York boroughs and started too many projects. I just overwhelmed myself with too much to do and too little time. My mother saw this in me. She saw I was starting to break down. Late one night as I cried to myself on the living room couch, mom approached me, sat with me and tried to tell me what I was doing to myself. She pointed out how I was attempting to accomplish more than humanly possible. She told me to tackle things that were most important to me first, and if I saw I had too many things to do, then whatever I couldn't handle I had to eliminate from my life. I follow that advice to this day. After our talk I started to feel much better. I removed all the things that burdened me mentally and felt relieved.

I made plans to see my buddy Robert who had joined the service with me and was now stationed in Connecticut on submarine duty. Old friends that I grew up with including Magoo, Carl "The Weapon," and myself decided we'd make an adventure of the trip. Carl earned the nickname The Weapon, because he always had something hidden nearby, so if we were in a rumble and outnumbered, which we always were, all we'd have to do was reach anywhere and he'd have something stashed. A club, stick, bat, chain, and a piece of wood, anything you could use as a weapon--it was there.

Magoo was the designated driver. We didn't want to take Carl's car. It was a '64 New Yorker and a tank. It was always breaking down and just a little too heavy to push. Magoo volunteered his Nova. We were to pick up Carl at 4 AM. We wanted to make an early start so we'd have a major part of the day to knock around on base with Robert.

We pulled up to Carl's house in the dark of morning. There was no Carl in sight. Magoo and I tried to figure out what we were going to do to get his attention. We didn't want to wake up the whole family. I started throwing pebbles at his bedroom window, but there was no response. Magoo and I looked at each other. Then Magoo said "Fuck it! We'll go without him."

So in the car we went, off to Connecticut. We bullshitted for a while as we drove along. Magoo said that it was Carl who wanted to leave early in the morning, and that he would have preferred to have slept a little longer. I asked him what time he went to sleep. He told me about 2 AM.

"So you only had two hours of sleep, if that?" I asked him.

Magoo shrugged, "Pretty much, but I'm all right. Why don't you snooze?"

I couldn't seem to doze off. After my car accident in the service, I developed a fear about falling asleep in the car.

We stayed quiet for a while. We started approaching the entrance to a bridge exiting New York. I was looking out the window when I realized Magoo was starting to veer left. As I turned my head I realized Magoo had fallen asleep at the wheel. I yelled out "Magoo!" startling him. But I was not quick enough to keep him from smashing into the tremendous lampposts right before the entrance of the bridge.

"Shit!" Magoo exclaimed as we jumped out to survey the damage. Magoo leaned down to look at the mess. I stood in front of the car peering at the mess. I felt a sensation, as if something was pushing me forward, when I heard a thunderous Boom!

With a loud crash, chards of splintering glass shot out in all directions as the glass dome from the three-story lamppost we'd hit came crashing down, just missing me by inches.

Amazed, Magoo said, "Wow, someone up there was watching over you!"

I shook my head, "Geeze, Magoo, if you don't get me killed today!"

The damage wasn't bad enough to keep the car from running, but Magoo was embarrassed and didn't want to continue on the rest of the trip. He didn't want to pull on base with the car looking the way it did, so we headed home. We made the trip another time after the Nova was fixed, and we were able to bring Carl with us on the second attempt.

The "Apostles" continued to do shows. We made the local papers and all was going really well. It was a good place in time for me. We had endless beach parties, parking under the Whitestone Bridge, submarine race watching. Everybody was just hanging out having a good time singing, and going to a lot of clubs and oldies rock 'n roll shows, seeing the old groups.

ROSE COLORED GLASSES

I was very/ attracted to Lizzie. We had good communication and spent hours on the phone at night when we weren't together. But, I was looking at a lot of things through rose colored glasses. I didn't see the signs of many things foreshadowing my future.

I went to pick her up Thanksgiving that year. It was her birthday. I sat in the living room waiting for her family to finish at the dinner table. Lizzie's father asked who would be cleaning up the Thanksgiving dinner mess. No one volunteered. Lizzie didn't, figuring her brothers would be nice and take care of the clean-up since it was her birthday. But the answer across-the-board was a chorus of "not me."

Well, the old man went into a rage the likes of which I had never witnessed in my family. He started to fling everything off the dining room table and into the kitchen. Glasses, dishes, food, including the uncarved turkey, went sailing through the air. I never saw a flying turkey before, especially not after it was cooked!

I closed my eyes to a lot of actions I witnessed at Lizzie's home. It was my nature to overlook. Lizzie tended to be moody and hypersensitive. She would take things that were meant to be funny and interpret them instead in a serious way, thereby overreacting to many petty things.

I recall a time we took my younger sister MaryAnn to the circus. Lizzie became very upset that someone was smoking pot nearby. She wanted me to do something about it. She created a lot of tension and ruined the day. Another time we took MaryAnn to the Museum Of Natural History. Again she got annoyed at something, refusing to speak to me or come into the museum, as my sister waited nervously. We never knew what made her angry. I was forced to take my little sister through the exhibits, while Lizzie sat and waited in the lobby, pouting.

This would be the trend with her. Everyone felt like we were walking on egg shells around her. She had a roller coaster personality. When she was not in a bad mood, she was great fun to be around. She was upbeat. The family came to really love her, and she was like a big sister to MaryAnn, taking her under her wing. She was very personable and talkative, but she could change on a dime. If Lizzie felt slighted by someone she quickly eliminated people from her life, whether they were family or friends, never to speak to them again or consider forgiveness.

Despite these little warning signs, I decided to marry her. It was Valentine's Day. I bought the largest heart-shaped box of chocolate candy I could find and hid a gorgeous engagement ring inside it. I cruised up to Central Park in the city with Lizzie and my '57 Coupe Deville. It was a picture-perfect February day. I pulled over to a picturesque spot, gave Lizzie the box of candy and asked her to marry me. It was a classic moment!

Although, we were doing most everything in the way of wedding preparations, I knew this would all be coming out of my pocket. Lizzie's father didn't have a penny. We did everything ourselves, with no one to help us. A few months before the wedding, Lizzie's father Al had found a nice apartment for himself and his sons to live. I helped with the move, of course. It poured rain all that day. We were all young, so the poor weather didn't stop her two brothers and I from going forward with the move. I did end up sick after getting soaked all day. With youth comes stupidity. I wasn't feeling well after the move, but I continued at work one day until I almost collapsed under the lifts with close to 104° fever. My dad was telling me "Why didn't you say something? Go home if you're feeling sick."

The way we were brought up, though, was that if you weren't dead and didn't see your name in the obituary in the morning, then you got up and you went to work. I had no choice now but to stay home.

I ended up with a severe case of walking pneumonia. No one was even sure I was going to make my own wedding. Then Lizzie started acting weird, telling me she was scared. I understood her fears and tried to reassure her everything would be all right. We were planning to live in Brooklyn since my job was there. I kept reassuring her she would love Brooklyn. It was a great place.

Although we were doing most everything on our own for the wedding, my mother Mary was hard at work. She felt bad that Lizzie was without her mother. She planned and gave her a beautiful surprise bridal shower. My mother was very good to her. But, it didn't take much to get Lizzie twisted. God forbid she could overlook something. She asked my mom to do her a favor and take her to her dressmaker for a final fitting of her wedding gown. I guess Lizzie had it in her head that nobody should see the dress until the church. By accident my mother saw her in it during the fitting. This enraged Lizzie beyond belief. I never heard the end of it. I told her, "What did you want my mother to do, stand outside in the rain. What's the big deal? It's only the groom that's not to see you ahead of time." She didn't want to hear of it and resented my mother, holding it against her, for seeing her in the dress!

That wasn't the only problem. She seemed to be having a lot of issues. Things were coming out of left field that had absolutely nothing to do with anything. We had a fight at one point and I'm not one to fight. It emotionally drains me and makes me physically sick. The argument got so bad I was walking out the door just about to leave her for good.

"Wait!" She said as I went to the door, "Don't go, it's me, and I know I'm thinking stupidly." What possessed me to stay, when I knew down deep I should have left, I don't know. Now to top it all off, Lizzie's father Al has an emphysema attack that lands him in the hospital. This is a guy that has oxygen tanks delivered to the house, has tubes up his nostrils. Yet, you'd walk into the house and find a cigarette hanging from his lips.

Now the pressure was on to finalize all last-minute wedding plans. Plus, Lizzie wanted to visit her father as often as she could. I would leave work from Brooklyn, head up to Queens, pick her up, visit her father, and then I'd drop her back off at her house. Finally I'd go back home. I didn't mind doing this, but the amount of times was ridiculous.

Lizzie also decided that after the ceremony at the church we would visit her dad before going to the catering hall. It was a nice gesture to let her dad see us all dressed while he was in the hospital. However, I'm sure we could have done it more easily at a different point in the evening instead of being pressed for time. We missed our entire cocktail hour, and the guests were getting restless for the festivities to start. It was not an enjoyable experience on my part.

One high note though, was that the Apostles got to sing a couple of songs at the reception.

I tried to make life as normal and romantic as possible as our life together began. It would be anything but normal. First we ended up taking my new bride's father's dog with us to our new apartment. He was a huge German Shepherd named Captain. Lizzie felt the boys weren't caring for the dog properly while her dad wasn't there. That made for a more difficult situation getting our first apartment. Not all landlords allowed pets. Myself? I'm not exactly an animal lover. Not that I don't like animals—they're fine as long as I don't have to be the one to care for them. I don't want to have to walk the dog before I go to work in the mornings or before I want to relax for the evening. Needless to say, it became my job once the dog was with us. I hated to be out in the rain and cold and snow!

Lizzie would coo, "Come on honey, please, do me a favor, you know I love you," and promises of her taking care of her dog went out the window quickly.

Lizzie had this thing about visiting her father every weekend even after he was out of the hospital. I used to beg her "can't we take a break! "I worked six days a week, long hours, a hard job, and my pleas of "have a little consideration for me" fell on deaf ears.

Lizzie started to get wind of stories from her brother Jerry that while we were busy setting up house and working, we seemed to have no time for our friends anymore. Lizzie felt that everyone was talking behind our backs. She insisted I call the guys from the group to my home and confront them with everything. It was so warped, but I did whatever it took to please her. She sat hidden in the closet as the guys arrived. Mike, Stevie, and Tommy, were close friends of mine besides being members of the Apostles. Lizzie insisted that I tell everyone where it was at, that true friends don't talk behind each other's backs. I sat there talking to them, holding Captain, our German shepherd by the neck. Not a pretty picture. I'm sure it looked very hostile, and I sounded that way from the way Lizzie had me keyed up. So it was goodbye to good friends. Lizzie wanted us not to have anything to do with anyone anymore. With that the Apostles singing together fell apart, and so did my friendships with them.

I believe this was the beginning of my losing control over my life. I continued to do whatever it took to make Lizzie happy even if I made myself sick doing it. Eventually, a letter came in the mail. I had gotten called in for a job with the US Post Office. I had taken the test the year before and applied for the postal job along with a number of other jobs, especially utility companies like Con Edison and Brooklyn Union gas. They all offered good benefits and I really didn't want to continue doing transmission work. I wanted a better life. The only ongoing problem was my failure to pass the physical exams because of my service-connected injuries. My brother Stevie had already been working for the post office for a few years and liked it. He said it was a good job with good benefits. So I in turn took the job.

Like anything in life you have to start at the bottom. They gave me the midnight shift, which created a series of battles between Lizzie and me. I work for the USPS a total of three weeks and then I quit. After all that time waiting to get called, which was an opportunity in and of itself, I just couldn't take Lizzie's arguing with me anymore about the hours. I was actually getting physically ill fighting with her every day. She pushed me beyond the limits, throwing things at me and spewing verbal slurs— constant fighting. She'd lock herself in the bathroom after flinging things at me, hitting me on the side of the head with a bar of soap, slicing my ear open. According to her, I was the crazy one after I'd punch my fist through the door and then knocked the pins out of the hinges, pulling the door off the frame. To Lizzie, everything was always my fault!

ONLY THE BEGINNING

She didn't like the hours I was working even though I told her it was temporary to begin with. She didn't want to hear it. She was afraid to stay by herself at night. I understood that, but I needed her to sacrifice a little for the good of both of us.

For months to come I anxiously remained in the apartment fearing my family would discover I wasn't working. Everyone thought I was working, and I knew I would catch hell from the family if they knew I had quit. We got by on Lizzie's bank teller pay and my veterans pension.

I finally broke the news to everyone after I had taken a job in the mailroom of Smith Barney, a financial company and big Wall Street firm. I didn't take long for me to be promoted to the head of the audiovisual department. I remained employed for a short time there also, maybe six months, with none of the pay increases promised. I found that with my travel and lunch costs, I could earn more money delivering groceries on a bicycle in Brooklyn. I made sure I told my boss that as I walked off the job.

It became increasingly difficult to find a job at that time in 1973. There were so many returning vets from the Vietnam War; there were few jobs available. I found another job working for Lumber Headquarters. They were looking for veterans to help them build their company. Long hours, hard work and poor conditions ensued. I even worked Easter Sunday. I wondered who would be doing home improvements that day. When I wasn't delivering lumber to strange locations, like paneling to the 9th floor of the projects, I was out in the lumber yard in all kinds of weather. I wasn't a happy camper.

Eventually I ended up back at Imperial Transmissions, dad's shop. My folk's tenants had just moved out and the upstairs apartment on E 19th St. was available. Mom and dad offered it to us allowing us to save money on rent. I could even go into work with dad, saving on travel expenses. Lizzie was hesitant about the move. I had to convince her it was m our best interest to move there.

We took the second floor apartment and started to decorate it. She informed me her dad was coming down from College Point to pay a visit. He would be showing me how to put up paper in the kitchen. Evidently he was feeling good because he never went anywhere. But I was dreading his lesson. His temperament was one of impatience and nastiness. I tolerated him for the sake of my wife. Needless to say, he had me a nervous wreck as I struggled to put up the wallpaper. That weekend after he had gone, I ripped everything down and redid the whole job, with my own finished project coming out beautifully.

Shortly after moving in Lizzie and I started fighting again. There was always a complaint. Mostly it was about my mother or grandmother who lived in the apartment across the hall. My folks had the first floor in the house I grew up in. Lizzie would get upset. My grandmother, whom we used to refer to as Nani, would knock on the door during the day to say hello in broken English, mostly in an Italian accent. Nani hardly spoke English and was just trying to be nice. I couldn't understand it. Even with my mother, Lizzie would be best of friends with her one day doing activities such as shopping or talking for hours. Then next thing I'd know she'd be complaining to me about things my mother said or did. If I tried to make light of it, I got the guilt trip of me siding with my mother, if I said I'll talk to mom about these things, she'd quickly stop me and tell me to not say anything!

To complicate life further we received the joyous good news Lizzie was pregnant with our first child. She became very chummy with my mother. For months mom took her back and forth to the doctor for her visits while I went to work. Yet, she always managed to bitch about something mom did or said when I got home. She would drive me crazy. Then she would threaten me with what she was going to do or say. I was easy going but after hours on end listening to her nag me and never listen to anything I would say to appease the situation, I would be riled to a point I wanted to punch her lights out.

In my shear frustration I found myself screaming at her to just shut up and do what I say! On one occasion of her endless ranting, I'd put my fist to her head giving her a noogie, but did not hit her at all. The next day when I came home from work, Lizzie told me she hadn't felt good all day and was feeling dizzy. I asked her if she wanted me to take her to the doctor. She felt it was probably the pregnancy and nothing to worry about. She became worse, though, and I insisted I'd take her to the doctor. I told her I was sorry and that maybe it was because I had taken my fist to her head. She insisted it wasn't and told me to not tell the doctor that story.

When we got to the doctor she had already made up a story for him about how she hit her head on the dresser as she was bending over cleaning. The doctor never believed a word of it. I knew from the way he had looked me in the eye. I never flinched and remained composed. The doctor said Lizzie was suffering from a concussion. I felt scared to death. I never realized how heavy handed I was and how fragile women were. I swore to her and to myself that it would never happen again, and it didn't.

We got past this as all things pass with time. Lizzie's demeanor calmed as she seemed to manage whatever was bothering her. Before we knew it, she was going into labor, which started in the middle of the night at about two o'clock in the morning. She wanted me to keep track of her labor pains so I started jotting down on paper the time and distance between contractions as I kept an ongoing log. What started at 2 a.m. that night became endless with no sleep. I, of course, rose from bed and went to work that day. On my return that night I found my mother and grandmother in the apartment with my wife. They were keeping vigilant track of everything at Lizzie's request.

I took over duties as mom and Nani went about their business. At some point during that evening Lizzie swore she was going to have the baby. Off we ran, as I drove calmly down Flatbush Avenue. Upon examining her, the doctor said she wasn't ready yet and sent us back home. Another sleepless night ensued as I tried to fulfill her request to continue logging her episodes of contractions. Once more off to work I went. By the time I arrived home that night, 1 was exhausted. I wondered when she would finally have the baby. Lizzie was at least able to take naps in between her labor pains, and I had no rest at all. Finally, at about 2:30 a.m., I drove frantically through the streets of Brooklyn, carefully scurrying through red lights and stop signs as Lizzie's contractions came two minutes apart. I almost thought I would have to carry her up the steps of the hospital.

They were ready for us as we entered the main doorway as medical staff whisked Lizzie away in a wheelchair up to the maternity floor. I had to wait in the lobby with my brother Stevie who had joined us by my mother's insistence so that I wouldn't be alone at the hospital. I think my mother realized how tired I was.

There were wooden benches in the lobby, and I couldn't see straight anymore.

No sooner had I fallen asleep when my brother shook me wildly. "Wake up, wake up, she had a boy, the guard told me!" I woke up in a stupor for not having slept for a few nights. My brother Stevie was excited. I felt dopey and foggy and in shock. We made the trip up to the maternity floor, and as we stepped off the elevator, nurses approached us with a baby in an incubator type of cart. The nurse announced, "You have a beautiful, healthy daughter!"

Daughter? I was stunned and looked at my brother Stevie, "I thought you said it was a boy!"

"I know, I thought that's what the guard said. I was having a hard time understanding him."

I didn't care. I was more than happy to look down and see this beautiful, wide-eyed little girl looking all around so inquisitively. I had really wanted a girl rather than a son. It seemed like most of my life was spent with males, and I welcomed the change. The nurse opened the lid of the bassinet, and I extended my hand into it as the baby reached up with her little hand and grabbed my pinky. Holding it, I was amazed at how aware she was for just having been born.

She was my first born! We were to name her Destiny in loving memory of my friend Eddie, whom I had been close to. I was a proud Daddy and actually felt guilty that I had to take a few days off from work to help Lizzie at the hospital and at home. Of course, I did all the traditional handing out of cigars which I think at that time was starting to become a passe tradition. I phoned everyone—friends and relatives— and related the good news. Everyone was ecstatic. I was soon to realize, however, that everything that should have been blissful would become a nightmare.

THE DEVIL SHOWS HIS FACE

Lizzie was busy setting rules for visiting and phone callers such as who should come or call, at what time would be good for her and the baby, who she was going to allow in to see Destiny and who she wasn't. Everything that should have been joyful became trauma drama. Lizzie became increasingly annoyed with friends and relatives stopping by with gifts wanting to offer good wishes and see the baby.

Everything seemed to peak as we made plans for Destiny's christening. My mother, of course, volunteered to help in any way she could and offered us the use of the basement apartment for the party. It was quite large and that was basically what the family used it for: holidays and special occasions. So we took her up on that since our apartment upstairs was small, and it would be rather crowded for a big gathering.

As the day of the event neared, Lizzie told me her father and her brothers Jerry and Alex would attend. They would be there early on the day of the christening. She wanted no one else there with her as she was dressing the baby. My mother and Nani were looking forward to this, as Destiny was their grand and great grandchild. It was an Italian tradition that the mothers and grandmothers be together as the baby was being dressed. This whole situation turned into a horror with me in the middle feeling torn as I realized that deliberately keeping my mother and grandmother away was hurting them.

Lizzie would have no part of my rationale to let my mom and Nani join us. I told her the men would stay in the other room and we'd make sure we kept out of her way. She couldn't deal with it and, ranting and raving, told me mom's a pain in the ass and always had to have her way. She shouted, "Now I'm going to have mine! You know what? I don't even want to use her basement. I don't want anything from that woman. Tell her we're having the party up here."

Now I really felt like hell. Upset beyond belief, I told my folks that we would not be using the basement for the party after all and that nobody was permitted to come upstairs while we were getting ready for church. The situation Lizzie created made for hard feelings on everyone's part. I remember feeling sick as we left the house dressed for church with everyone finally seeing the baby bundled as we were walking out. It was very phony trying to be pleasant on Lizzie's part while at the door. As we walked away from the house and headed toward the church, it felt like a day from hell filled with the devil. I dreaded the entire rest of the day. I apologized to the Lord, in church, for feeling this way on a day that should have been blessed.

When we returned home after services our apartment filled with all our guests held a strange uneasiness. It was hard trying to get through the day pretending to feel joyous and party-like.

My Aunt Ann had arrived. She was my brother Stevie's godmother. She wanted to peek at the baby while Destiny had fallen asleep on our bed surrounded by guests' coats and pillows.

Lizzie, of course, stated that she didn't want the baby disturbed and closed the bedroom door. The older Italians thought it was not a big deal to quietly whisper and sneak into the bedroom to peer at the baby. Lizzie became enraged at Aunt Ann and gave her the most evil look imaginable, as if she wanted to kill her.

My Aunt Ann said to my mother, "Oh my God, did you see the way she looked at me!" Lizzie went from enraged to hysterical as she pulled me into the bathroom with her, unleashing her fury at me. She became so out of control that I lightly smacked her face to shake her out of it.

I told her she ruined the day for everyone.

"This stops right now! Stop it, stop it. Do you hear me?" in a low but stern voice, I walked out of the bathroom, leaving her standing there with her mouth open.

Life seemed to continue down the same path as we lived upstairs from my parents. It was very erratic. There were days when Lizzie was everyone's best friend and days she was their enemy and despised them.

One evening the doorbell rang. I answered it to find my friend Kevin looking for his wife Lisa, whom we used to call "little Queenie." She was a young mother who had a baby out of wedlock when she was 15. But Kevin did the right thing and married Lisa. He was a good kid still in his teens, too. "Bobby, have you seen Lisa?"

"No, Kevin, we haven't seen her. What's wrong?"

Kevin explained that they had a fight. Lisa threatened to take the baby and leave him. He was beside himself. I tried to reassure him not to worry, that she probably went to her mother's for a few days and maybe she just needed a little cooling off period. I told him if he was really worried I'd help him look for her.

He assured me it wasn't necessary and that he was okay. He thought he knew where she might be. I didn't hear from Queenie or Kevin for the next couple of weeks. Then I received a call from a mutual friend telling me that they had found Kevin's body boarded up in his living room, sitting in a beach chair with a can of beer in his hand. His head hung down and a barbeque grill was sitting next to him. The stench and the maggots flying out his second floor apartment window was what alerted the neighbors and authorities.

I was in shock and related the story to Lizzie, hoping it would impact her to realize how short life was and that she should try not to make issues out of small and meaningless things. In the scheme of life these issues were trivial and not worth fighting about.

It was to no avail. As life moved forward she ended up at odds with my mother again. One evening my mother and father came up together to see if we could calmly talk together to find out what the issues were. After all, we were family and mom and dad felt that anything could be overcome for the sake of family. It ended with Lizzie screaming at the top of her lungs at my mother to get out of her house- My poor folks walked out in disbelief. I sat in disbelief. For quite some time my trips to work with dad in the car were very tense as we both sat quietly on our way to the shop.

I realized that Lizzie was just plain resentful of living in what she considered my folks' house. I looked at the house on East 19th Street as being mine. It was the home I grew up in. But I had to end all this friction for everyone's sake, especially mine. 1 felt sick emotionally and let my folks know we'd be moving out by the end of the month. I'm sure as much as they thought they were helping us out they were glad to see us go. I pressured myself to find an apartment in a hurry.

We took an apartment on 10th St. between Ave. N and O. It was considered to be part of the Midwood section of Brooklyn. It was mostly a Jewish community with many Hasidic Jews. I had no problem living there, but I took exception to the way many Hassidic did not seem to mingle with others outside of their own people. They would not even allow their own children to approach my Destiny.

This was our third apartment I was going to spend time and money fixing. Lizzie and I liked to have things feeling like home and looking presentable. I believed we would settle in and never foresaw our time here would be short. I started to doll the place up, but Lizzie took a lot for granted.

I also convinced Lizzie she'd have to learn to drive now. My mom wasn't going to be around to take her everywhere she wanted to go. I taught her to drive and bought her a car, but nothing made her happy. She was always complaining about something. At any point during her ranting and raving she always managed to throw my mother into the equation.

One day after about 3 hours of badgering me, I couldn't take it anymore. I was in the bedroom when I flipped out, striking the wall with my fist, leaving the impression of my fist there. She continued with senseless hysterics about my mother, family and whatever she let bother her, which was anything and everything. I continued attacking the wall until I finally landed a blow that sent my fist sailing through the bedroom wall and into the living room.

She screamed "OK, OK! Take it easy!"

Fuming, I answered, "You just don't ever stop, do you?" I gazed at the half dozen holes I had put into the wall knowing that I now had to repair them. I glanced at my hand that was swelling with skinned knuckles that were starting to bleed. I looked at Lizzie as she glared at me.

"You know I have to work with these hands!" I shouted at her, but there was no comment from her, and that ended that commotion.

She was never satisfied until I went over the edge. Things just got worse in this new apartment. One problem led to another. After never-ending decorating and home improvements, we started to have a water bug problem. The huge, black slippery bugs were coming out of their hiding spots and making their presence known all over the apartment.

We were concerned for the baby. Lizzie would seem to notice a water bug at bed time. She'd become hysterical and would never let me sleep until I found and killed it. I was disgusted by them also. They were huge. I'd never seen bugs as big as this; they'd fly! I couldn't believe they had wings. If the house was quiet you could hear them walking across the kitchen linoleum. The landlord never did anything about them until I started leaving paper bags outside his upstairs door filled with the ones I had killed.

My anger at the landlord's ignoring our bug infestation was multiplied by not having heat supplied to us all winter. I'd march up to his door to complain. The landlord and his wife would be sitting on their couch bundled up in sweaters and blankets. Then they'd tell me "Oh, you should have heat since you're near the boiler room."

Staring stonily at them I'd said, "Well, if the boiler went on once in a while maybe we'd feel warm." I'd storm away angrily. I finally had a battle with the landlord after I replaced a broken entry door lock. He insisted on having the new key, and I refused to give it to him. I thought we might go to blows, but we didn't. Considering the bugs, no heat, and Destiny turning blue from the cold, I knew once again it was time to move on.

SHADOWS

I learned to take a little more time in finding the right apartment. I decided not to jump into something I didn't know and not to pressure myself with a time commitment. I didn't say we were moving until we found the right apartment. My instincts were correct; I found the perfect place.

It was the entire top floor of a large house at the end of Gravesend Neck Road. It was a beautiful bright spacious apartment. It was perfect for us, classy and up to date. The family that owned the home loved us, and we were happy with them. They were very nice, down to earth Italian people that had traditional values. Once again I upgraded another apartment with cleaning, painting, and decorating. The kindly landlord was excited that I was painting the entire apartment since the previous tenants before us hadn't done much to improve the place.

Life is never smooth sailing. We started off there with an episode with Destiny. It was grueling. Our baby girl, not quite two years of age yet, was getting into trouble at every turn. One day she pulled out all the drawers on her dresser, climbed to the top and stood. With the balance of the weight leaning forward, we heard a scream and a crash from her bedroom that sent us running at rapid speed to see what had happened. The dresser had toppled over with Destiny having flown off, though she was unscathed. Without her even shedding a tear, we picked her up and held her for dear life.

As brave as we thought she had been, on the second night after the fall, Destiny wandered into our bedroom, shaking and scared to death, unable to sleep. She told us she was seeing shadows. She explained in her own little way that everything was moving. Lizzie and I and Destiny began a week of what was to become unexplained horror.

My baby would cling to me in a total panic, fear-stricken. She kept saying things and we didn't understand what was going on inside her mind. Lizzie and I took turns trying to get some sleep and rest. Destiny had not slept now for more than four days. She was so petrified one evening; she imagined that the print on my pajamas was coming alive. I stood in place in the middle of the kitchen, completely disrobed, and held onto her for hours until Lizzie woke up and took my place.

The next day my mom and dad came over to help. My mother concocted some holy oils and garlic mix. She was going through the house from room to room blessing them. This was an old Italian remedy, I presumed. Whatever it was, it actually worked! Destiny finally fell asleep out of sheer exhaustion. It was our chance to get some rest also. We decided to take her to the hospital emergency room when she awoke. We didn't know what else to do.

As it turned out they realized that Destiny was in shock from the fall. We should've patted her bottom even though we were concerned she'd hurt herself. This would have forced her to shed tears and prevented her from going into shock. She should have been crying. On top of that Lizzie was giving her some medication for chest congestion from a little cold she picked up from the last apartment. Between the shock of the fall and this particular medication, she was hallucinating. Gradually with the right steps taken we were all able to get back to normal.

Normal? In my home nothing was ever normal. Lizzie soon informed me how her brothers had abandoned her father Al, and he couldn't live alone. He needed daily care, so he'd have to move in with us. I wanted no part of it, but I figured for her sake what could I do?

Where would we put him? I knew this would be nothing but interference in our young lives. Lizzie decided to move her dad into Destiny's bedroom. Just what a two year old baby needed to be exposed to him lying in his bed all day, watching horror movies, surrounded by oxygen tanks and breathing machines. I was seeing the beginning already of an unnatural childhood for Destiny. Lizzie gave her dad the new bed we were going to use for Destiny. It was time for her to come out of her crib, but now, she was forced to stay in it. She watched as her mother doted on her grandfather. Many a night I would come in from work and find Destiny on his lap watching horror movies, not such nice visions for two-year-old!

Along with the craziness that went on with his stay at our apartment we had our own issues to contend with. Destiny was a very hyperactive child who ran us ragged, but we loved her dearly. Lizzie wanted more children, but she miscarried quite a number of times

I ended up with a hernia operation from lifting heavy transmissions all the time. My back was always going out and causing me to be laid up. I forced myself to go to work with my back out anyway. I could never afford to take a day off. There was no paid sick time in my occupation. On top of that, I kept getting called for jury duty. There was never a dull moment. For some reason, as I look back now, we seemed to be happiest in that apartment out of all our years together.

Then my grandmother, Nani passed away. She had lived a full life and we would miss her dearly. She was a big part of our family. Sometimes as the old timers fade away, families start to change. I have to hand it to my mother because she kept everyone together with the traditions and gatherings for years to come.

As soon as we thought life might finally settle down, my landlady approached me and announced that she found the house of her dreams. She would be putting this house up for sale.

The real estate recommended we would be wise to look for a new home as we might have to leave They had a buyer interested who wanted to give the rental apartment to someone in their family. She suggested we might want to look for a house of our own also

DIVINE INTERVENTION

We were shocked and didn't know what to do. We had so much to think about We really weren't financially in a position to buy a home. I despised the thought of starting over again in another apartment. We had her father to worry about. I didn't know what to do at first.

Somehow, divine intervention made things work out. Lizzie's dad had a bad emphysema attack and needed to be hospitalized, Her brother Jerry's personal situation changed. He needed to lean on his father and his Social Security money. When Al came out of the hospital, Jerry found a place to live together with his father. My dad came to the rescue and told us he'd help us out with a down payment for a house. We'd repay him down the road. Thus began the house hunting chapter of our lives.

We found a great house in Midwood. It was one of those things where you just know this is your place. You feel it. This is it! The home had a lot of potential; it was never really modernized. It had all the solid attributes of a house built in 1923. It was great! We bargained with the owner getting the house for $43,000, down from $49,500. With what I had saved and the $11,000 from my dad, we had the one-third down payment plus closing costs.

It was now 1976, and we had more than just the nation's Bicentennial to celebrate. We had a $243 a month payment for mortgage, taxes, and water and sewer bills. Things would be tight as I was only bringing home $200 a week.

As fate would have it, Lizzie now became pregnant with our second child. I knew I'd have to ask for a raise or things would become impossible. I was able to squeeze out of the boss's a $25 a week raise. Sometimes I really had to wonder whether or not I was doing the right thing working for my father. I knew that it wasn't dad holding back an increase; it was his partner who was cheap.

I started to work on the house. There was so much we wanted to do. Money was tight. We only had the necessities, kitchen table and bedroom furniture for ourselves and Destiny. The house and its rooms would stay empty for many years to come.

I stood looking out the kitchen window, "Wow, looks like a bad storm today." it was a good day for working around the house, I thought to myself. As I tapped a small screwdriver across my cheek, the phone rang.

Lizzie answered it. "It's your mother she wants to say hello". She handed me the phone.

"HI mom," we started to gab, when suddenly a thunderous crack of lightning struck the house. An instantaneous flash of bright light filled the room. The house lights went black, and Lizzie let out a scream, I saw an ark of current bursting from the phone receiver striking my mouth and the small screwdriver I held at my cheek. The force knocking me off the chair suddenly, it was as if someone had just round housed punched me.

As the lights came back on I looked up from the prone position across the kitchen floor. I held my mouth as I glanced at the telephone mounted in the wall recess which once mounted the house ironing board. The phone was melted to the wall and smoldering. Smoke was emanating from the dangling receiver. I could feel my mouth swelling as I stood up. I had a nice fat lip, but I was okay. Lizzie stood there repeating, "oh my God, oh my God! "

We didn't understand why this happened. We checked all our phone extensions in the rest of the house, realizing our whole system was down. We needed to call the phone company, so we had to use a neighbor's phone.

That Monday about mid-day, the shop phone rang. It was a call for me. My wife let me know that we had service again and that the incident was going to be investigated by Bell telephone service. She told me the serviceman said, "Your husband is lucky to be alive! " He told her that when they installed our phone system it was never grounded. That's what allowed current to be conducted through the phone system during the lightning strike.

The company called and spoke to me a few days later. They inquired if I was all right. I assured them I was. The representative told me that the person that installed the system was fired and once again told me I was very lucky. They continued with telephone inquiries throughout the following year. I gathered they were concerned not only about my welfare, but whether I had a lawsuit in mind. I told the representative I wasn't going to pursue legal action, I was only too glad to be alive. I thanked my guardian angel!

Soon after this incident, Lizzie gave birth. We had another beautiful little girl whom we named Lorrie. With a new baby in the house, Destiny still continued her mischievous ways. She was hyperactive and always wanted to be the center of attention. It seemed like we were constantly scolding her to be quiet. She was at us constantly and never stopped talking.

Lorrie as an infant was very easy. The only problem was that she teethed for two years. With never a tooth breaking through, the doctor thought he might have to lance her gums. She seemed to finally get past all that. Those sleepless nights were the hard part. Lizzie was very disgruntled about getting up for her and would end up waking everyone else with her ranting. I found it easier to just get up myself and take care of Lorrie. You certainly can't get a baby to sleep if you're nervous and tense. The baby would sense that in her mother and scream and cry even more. I purposely would return to bed and say "I don't know, I don't have a problem with her." it troubled me that Lizzie seemed to have no patience for her own child and no motherly instincts. I think it irked her that I could calm Lorrie and put her back to sleep. Of course Lizzie wouldn't give me any credit for my success with Lorrie.

Despite my belief that life rolled along fairly smoothly, I realized I couldn't see my situation was not really a normal one. I grew accustomed to a different kind of normal, and I never understood how truly dysfunctional my household was until years later when I took a step back as an outside observer and looked into the life I'd led.

Basically, we were doing a tremendous amount of running around. It was a very stressful lifestyle that we were leading. We were running constantly to Queens to take care of Lizzie's father. Sometimes she would even pick me up straight from work. I'd eat dinner out of a container while she was driving.

I think my kids suffered, too. The time and attention they deserved as children they didn't get. Every Sunday morning her brother Jerry would come by at 8 AM with donuts for breakfast. It's nice once in a while, but I asked Lizzie, "Can't you talk to your brother and ask him not to come by so often? I'm working six days a week very long hours, I'm exhausted. I could use one morning to get a little extra sleep. As a matter of fact, the kids and the whole household could use a calm morning once in a while!"

Her answer was "he's my brother. He can come if he wants too." The problem was she felt obligated to do things for others, She hated doing it and ended up taking it out on me. There was no thought or consideration for me or the kids. Many times we were leaving the girls with somebody to baby sit as we ran to visit her father in the hospital.

Life in my house always seemed like living on the edge. The next decade would only greet more turmoil.

NEVER A DULL MOMENT

Lizzie took a fall down the stairs and to avoid Lorrie getting hurt, whom she was holding, she bruised her breast against the bannister. She sustained an injury that needed medical attention for the month. I would pack her wound, sterilize and bandage her. With all our business Lizzie still wanted another child. She had suffered many miscarriages but insisted on still trying to become pregnant. She then suffered an atopic pregnancy, which almost became life threatening, as she was bleeding internally. There was a lengthy recovery period when she came home from surgery. She could not climb the stairs for some time, so we set up our empty dining room to be a bedroom.

I cared for her and the girls round the clock with constant trips up and down the steps to take care of them. My Aunt Nancy, my father's sister, started to volunteer to help so I could return to work after taking off a week from work. She would come with food or cook at the house taking care of everyone during the day. I was very grateful.

In the evenings I would drive my Aunt back home to Bensonhurst. She had her own family to take care of. In about a month's time I thought we would return to a more normal routine. Lizzie was able to use the stairs again, and we set the house back in order.

That night as I lie in bed my right knee was aching in pain. By the time I got up in the morning my old service injury had blown up like a balloon. I couldn't walk. I knew that the extra activity of the past five weeks climbing the stairs continuously had done me in.

I grabbed the baseball bat that I used to keep beside the bed. I needed something to lean on. I hobbled into the Brooklyn VA Hospital. I saw a doctor that concurred I had some major trauma to my knee and would have to be examined tomorrow by the head orthopedic man. They sent me back home, baseball bat and all.

It wasn't until I went back again the next day that they gave me a cane and set me up for surgery, the operation was to take place in the middle of November. I was set to go and couldn't wait to have it taken care of. The VA and Navy always fought with me about the knee, claiming I didn't have a problem with it, because they were worried I was only looking for compensation. Now they would perform arthroscopic surgery and remove the cartilage. Also, repair any other damage they found.

The week prior to going in the hospital my mother asked to have the family for Thanksgiving. It was family tradition that the entire family, all sides, would gather at moms for the day. It would be her holiday with the whole family.

I discussed it with Lizzie before we answered. "Are you sure you want to go? I'm going to have my leg in a cast and won't be able to help too much with the girls and getting out of the house."

Her response was, "No problem. I can do it. I want to go. I won't have any problems, don't worry, we'll be fine. I'm going to tell your mother we'll be there."

After staying with me the day of surgery and visiting me the next, Lizzie called me up that evening at the hospital and told me, "You know you have to be out of there this week. We're going to your mother's next week for Thanksgiving. What did the doctor say?"

I told her I didn't know and would have to see how I progressed through the week. Now she was stressing me to get out of the hospital quickly. That was up to the doctor, but she didn't want to hear it. "You tell them you have to be out of here!" I yessed Lizzie to death as her pressure on me was upsetting me.

Thank God I was feeling great. It was the best my knee had felt since I got hurt in the military. I was even surprised that after major surgery I hardly felt any pain there.

My wife continued to call me all day long every day telling me she'd been arguing with my mother over whether we were showing up for Thanksgiving. I didn't understand what the problem was. If I wasn't out in time, we wouldn't go. I didn't know what the big deal was. I guess it was too much for her to think about—how she was going to get out of the house with two kids and an incapacitated husband. I told Lizzie if it's too much for her we wouldn't make Thanksgiving.

"No, no, no, you don't understand. I told her we were still going when she spoke to me on the phone. You know how your mother is. She whines like a baby if she doesn't get her way." I think the problem was Lizzie feeling obligated once she had opened her mouth.

I told her I didn't care; we didn't have to go. Anyway, what was the big deal? The girls were not that hard to get ready. There was nothing she could do for me. I'd take care of myself. All she had to do was get herself ready and dressed. She fought with me for the next week about this over and over, making the whole situation more confusing than it really was.

Then, the day approached—Thanksgiving morning. We finally had a war as I couldn't take anymore of her bullshit. I was using crutches, the girls were ready, and now Lizzie said she didn't want to go as she cursed my mother and my family. She went on and on about how my mother had to have her way and she shouldn't have told her we were going. She didn't really want to go to begin with.

I couldn't take any more of her badgering so I told her, "So that's what the problem is! You know what, we're not going. I'll call right now and tell my mother I'm not up to it and we'll do it another time." Now she started cursing that I was always on my mother's side and I was a no-good fuck. She did nothing but have fights with her mentally. No matter what I tried to do to remedy the situation she was not happy. She got me so enraged I started hitting things across the dining room with my crutches.

"Know what? Cut the shit already, the fucking day is ruined as usual. Let's go,

I've had enough. Let's go, girls." I called Destiny, Lizzie took the baby and we hustled out the door, all of us in angry moods, which was par for the course!

DIFFERENT DIRECTION

Time progressed and we went on in our usual way, constantly struggling to make ends meet. I did side work whenever possible and always seemed to bail us out of whatever financial jam we were in. The more I did the more I contemplated opening my own business. I never felt we had enough money to start my own shop. I had put a claim in to the Veteran's Administration for an increase in compensation and possibly reward retroactive for my knee injury. Like all bureaucracies this was going to take time to achieve

We continued to carry on a hectic lifestyle, which was basically our own doing, because we constantly ran back and forth to Queens, NY, for Lizzie's father and family.

It was the early 80's and Lizzie wanted another child, which I had no problem with, but I also knew I needed to make more money to keep the family growing and living decently. I knew I couldn't continue on the amount of funds I was bringing in. I decided to ask for a raise at work.

My father's partner Benny seemed to be the one I had to ask. I knew my dad had no problem with me making more money. He knew I deserved it, and when I mentioned it, he told me to get Benny's okay. I was shocked at the answer I got from Benny. I got a halfhearted $25.00 a week increase, and he told me "How far do you think you're going to go with our shop? You should think about taking the city test!"

I couldn't believe my ears. I had worked for my dad and him now for 15 years. They were long, hard hours, lots of overtime without pay, never much in the way of rewards or bonuses, except for one Christmas my dad insisted on giving his employees $500. 1 think Dad offered this mostly because he knew my pneumatic air gun was stolen, and it was going to cost me a couple of hundred dollars to buy another.

The way Benny had posed it to me was like saying why don't you ask the guy across the street for a job? I was stunned. I had put my heart and soul into my father's shop since I had started for him. I was very upset about the whole thing. When I spoke to my dad about it, he told me not to worry and to do what was best for me. He'd understand and I shouldn't feel guilty about it.

First chance I'd gotten, I picked up a number of civil service papers and filled out applications. To everyone's surprise I followed through, took all the tests and was number two on the list for the Department of Sanitation mechanic. No one expected this as I had no formal training in auto mechanics. It was strictly on the job training. Not that it was a prestigious position, but it was time to move on with my life and leave dad's shop. I had believed I'd have some sort of future there someday but that wasn't to be the case. The city called me. Like any job I started all over again at the bottom with the midnight shift. This was basically what I considered monkey work and maintenance and nothing really challenging. Also from working in East New York, now I had to take a ride to Bushwick, which was not the best of neighborhoods. I'd stop at a light and the rats would be playing in the street at midnight.

A number of months went by. I realized this job wasn't for me. I was itching for normal again. I couldn't get used to the late shift. I never slept and I ate day and night. The money wasn't the greatest either. I made the sacrifice to get my foot in the door but it wasn't working out. I ended up quitting, going back to transmission work, but not for my father's shop anymore. I started to make more money right off the bat and realized how underpaid I was for so many years. I also learned that times were changing and it didn't pay to stay at one job too long. The only way to get ahead was to keep moving, advancing myself and my pay scale.

I met a fellow, Eddie, at one job who seemed to be a very good and conscientious guy willing to learn the right way of doing things. We started doing a lot of side work together. At one point we had both quit our jobs and started working in back of my house pulling transmissions out in my driveway on our backs and rebuilding them in my garage. We did all kinds of general repairs, too.

We were doing quite well and then the realization of winter weather came down upon us. We talked about what we were going to do and decided we'd go back to work for someone. Then in the spring I'd look to make connections and start our own shop. This didn't go over very well with Lizzie when it finally came down to making the move. She insisted it was the wrong time to go into business as she was pregnant with our third child. I understood her concerns and reassured her not to worry. I'd been in the trade long enough. I knew what I was doing, and I had a great reputation. She didn't want to hear it. It became another thing to argue about day and night. She really knew how to drain a person of their drive and motivation. So like everything I ever did, I went against the grain, always being emotionally sick with whatever I was attempting to do.

Eddie and I opened shop in the fall of 1983. My VA claim had finally come through, and I had received $5,000 retroactive compensation check. I came up with my 5K and Eddie did, too. I had $800 in savings and figured it was emergency money.

Lizzie gave birth in October to our third beautiful little girl whom we named Eva. But, Lizzie seemed to lose her mind through each pregnancy with hormones and postpartum depression. She was driving me crazy. Things got so bad at home she told me, "Don't come home! Fuck you, I don't want you here!"

I was exhausted working from 7 AM in the morning until midnight to try to get the business going, then I'd come home late to her bitching and try to help with the baby during the night, but nothing was good enough. Yes, things were rough. We didn't take any money home for six months, and our first pay check was for $75. We kept putting anything we made right back into the business. She just kept on fighting with me.

I couldn't take it anymore and started sleeping in the shop. I'd stay days at a time, and she didn't give a damn. I'd felt like all I did was breathe in fumes from all the chemicals we used, and I always felt oily and dirty. I would actually sneak into the house when I knew she'd be out with the kids just to shower and clean up after days with no fresh clothes or bathing. I was always sick to my stomach.

On top of this I was starting to see a pattern with my partner Eddie. He was slacking off wanting to play boss while I carried the place. He had more reasons not to show up or leave early than I could think of. One day my dad actually slipped into the shop to help me out as I was all alone. I couldn't even find good help to hold onto. My father knew what I was going through. Even though he was concerned that his partner wouldn't be happy with my dad's presence in my shop, he didn't care. But as we worked together dad said, "Please, son, don't get this girl pregnant again. She's off the wall normally and when she has given birth to a child she's completely insane. Please, this is all tearing the family apart knowing what's going on."

I told him, "I know, don't worry. It's not going to happen again. This is it!"

The following weekend Lizzie was so off the wall and not thinking, she took the girls and our newborn, got in her girlfriend Karen's car with no brakes, and headed into the Pocono Mountains. I was so angry.

I'd typically do anything to avoid fighting, but I gave her hell when she got back. I couldn't believe what she had done, but she thought it was no big deal. She also suddenly stated that she wanted to go back to work.

"What are you kidding me? Who's going to take care of the baby? You wanted a baby, and now you want to go back to work. You don't even spend any time with the other girls. You volunteer for everything and you have time for nothing."

Defiantly, Lizzie said, "I have a life too, you know!"

"You wanted a family and that comes first," I shot back. I just didn't get her anymore.

VOICE FROM THE PAST

We sat eating dinner one evening. The phone rang and Lizzie answered it. "Oh my God, it's Mike! " Mike, my old friend whom we had lost ties with, found me and got in touch after 10 long years.

"What do you say we get together with the guys and their families? Maybe we can hit some notes or even put something together again!" he said to me. I got very excited at the fact of maybe singing again and that my old friend, whom I had been very close to, had gotten in touch with me. I ran the idea by Lizzie to have them all visit. It would be a nice reunion and to see everyone's kids and where they all were 10 years later. Lizzie was fine with it, as she had been friends with everyone also.

We set a date and waited with anticipation to see everyone. I was very, very excited about the thought of maybe putting the old group back together. Mike and I always felt like the music was in our blood.

Everyone seemed to arrive at the same time. It was a happy moment as they came through the door. Mike came with his wife Marion who was very nice and down to earth. His two daughters, Kelly and Laura, were cute and my girls' ages. Mike's brother Stevie and Donna had tied the knot with three boys in tow.

Tom and his wife Patti walked in last. Seeing Tom was a shock. He had changed the most physically. He had lost a lot of weight. He had become diabetic. This didn't surprise me. He was a short order cook and loved to eat. Patty's family was old fashion Italian and ate very heavy foods. They would do the whole 9 yards for dessert every night, pastries and all. Diabetes was inevitable for Tom, if he didn't watch himself.

The evening went very well. We were all having a great time reminiscing. We talked about the old days of singing. Then we decided to see what we could still do together. The kids were having a great time downstairs playing. We started to do some harmonies in my empty dining room. It was perfect for a little echo.

Whew! Yeah! We still had it. It was still there. The blend of voices that we had between us, the sounds just seem to come so naturally to us. It was like second nature. We discussed the possibility of rehearsing every week and putting The Apostles back together again.

At this point Lizzie grabbed me alone, as we friends were speaking and took me to the foyer near the basement steps, where she was headed to reprimand the kids for running up and down. Whispering sternly to me, she stated, "If you think this is gunna fucking go on every week, you can forget it, do you hear! I'm not having this go on here and not with them. Forget about singing, you've got enough to do!"

My heart sank quickly and my stomach churned. I felt sick. I went back to the guys and told them I would let them know. I felt like my change in mood killed the evening. Everybody sensed it, as I'm sure they saw it in my face. I told myself I'd better forget the whole idea of singing also. As disheartened as I felt, I didn't want another thing to be fighting about with my wife. I knew in my heart The Apostles would never be and I should just forget about singing. It saddened me. Even with my trying to convince Lizzie that after this evening's gathering there would only be rehearsals with the guys and not the kids, she wanted no part of it and my desire to sing meant nothing to her.

Nevertheless, the guys and I continued to stay in touch. Life was ironic. Things are either meant to be or they are not. I found that God acts in mysterious ways. Stevie and Donna moved to North Carolina. Stevie's company had moved there. He had a good position with the company and it was a wise move. Mike's lifestyle gave him no free time. Eventually, he worked four jobs and his wife Marion worked full-time in the supermarket butcher shop. Mike's mother was raising the girls. He had everything you could want in life, but no time to enjoy it. He and Marion eventually became like strangers in the night. Saddest of all was Tom. He eventually was hospitalized because of his diabetes. They started amputating his toes. Eventually he lost his balance and broke his hip. Complication on top of complication, Tommy never left the hospital. Mike called me and told me, "Bobby, Mr. Baseman is gone!" I was stunned. He was a young man yet. He just couldn't change his fate. It was very sad.

BACK TO REALITY

I continued to run myself ragged. The business was draining me. I couldn't get good and responsible help and had a partner I couldn't rely on. Problems at home never ceased. I couldn't continue the running I was doing for my father-in-law so we took him in. He lived in the middle of my empty dining room. We set a bed up, TV, and his oxygen tanks. With his wheelchair he rolled in and out of my kitchen constantly ruining my dinners by adding thyme to whatever my wife was cooking. I decided to refinish my basement and make an apartment for him down there. It was to be wheelchair accessible and everything built to accommodate his needs.

I was starting to get close to finished. Miserable as he always was, he actually seemed happy, having something to look forward to. But, like I said, God works in mysterious ways. Two weeks prior to my finishing his apartment, he had a major emphysema attack. The ambulance took him back to a hospital in Queens that his doctor was affiliated with. Lizzie and I started running back and forth to see him every day. Finally we returned home only to get a call to come back to the hospital. Al was not doing well. Within an hour of our returning he expired. It was as if the Lord didn't want him until he was happy!

Life goes on. Things change yet they remain the same. I would come home from work drained. I always looked forward to seeing my girls. I usually needed a little settle in time as I came through the door. It seemed a lot of things changed from when I was a kid. When my dad was about to get home, my mother would tell us to settle down, "Quiet! Your father will be home soon! He works hard all day; don't let him come in to a crazy house!"

Now I would come in and, like girls, screaming was an entrance hymn. Lizzie would look at me and say "They're yours now," like it was the changing of the guard. I dealt with it as best I could. I would feel guilty sometimes for yelling at them, but I never got a chance to wind down from work. Now I know why a lot of guys stop and hit the bar or whatever. They never seem to rush right home. I had no vices. I didn't smoke, drink, or stop to gamble. I went to work and came home.

If it wasn't the girls acting up, Lizzie would be angry at me for something or other. It seemed like everything was blamed on me. I came home one night, kissed the girls hello, walked into the kitchen, and said, "HI hon!"

She'd turn around and gave me an evil look. "What's the matter now?" I'd ask, sensing her anger with me.

"If you don't know, I'm not telling you!"

Muttering to myself, I'd think, "Here we fucking go." Later my oldest daughter Destiny approached me and said, "I know why she's mad at you, daddy!"

"Why, Destiny?"

"The pot boiled over on the stove today and there was a big mess. She told me this is your father's fault!" Unbelievable!

"You're kidding!"

"No, daddy, that's what happened and she's been mad all day."

You can't make this stuff up. It's what I lived through constantly. So as usual I was in the dog house: Silent treatment, coldness, tension in the air was the norm until the next bug got up her ass.

Lizzie approached me about Eva having a slight fever. "What should I do? I want to take her to the doctors."

I told her that she'd taken her to the doctors a half a dozen times already this winter, to just leave her alone, she'd be fine. The kids run a fever one day and the next day it's gone and they're up playing again. She felt all right to me; just leave her be.

Lizzie's response to me was, "I don't know why I ask you, you're just a cheap fuck! All you're worried about is the money!"

"No, 1 don't give a damn about the money. I just don't think you need to put her through anything she doesn't need. The kids get something one day and it's gone the next. Give it a day or two and see what happens with the fever—if it gets worse or if it goes away. It's a low grade fever, isn't it?"

Lizzie stormed, "I'm taking her NOW!"

"Do whatever you want; I don't know why you ask me."

On her return she told me the doctor had prescribed Ceclor to be taken ten days. Eva tested positive for strep throat. This was the fifth time this season. The poor kid! I felt for her. It turned out that the next day after the doctor visit, yes, and Eva's fever was gone and she was back to normal like I had figured.

As winter came to a close we started planning a vacation down to Florida to visit Lizzie's aunt who lived in Inverness. We figured we'd spend some time, take the kids to Disney, and maybe the change of scenery would help our relationship, too.

After her father had passed she started taking in stray pets on top of everything else that we had going on. I agreed to her taking in these dogs that other people didn't want, because Lizzie and the girls would beg and promise to take care of them, walking, feeding, cleaning up after, etc. None of the dogs she brought in were house broken.

Nevertheless, somehow I was the one walking the animals at midnight in the rain, the cold, the snow! In the mornings I had no time and I'd have to clean the kitchen of excrement and urine until I couldn't take it anymore. I told Lizzie to get rid of the dogs if they couldn't be trained. They were destroying the house, the house that I was trying desperately to fix up in what little spare time I had. I finally started leaving the mess in the morning. It seemed that was the only way to get Lizzie's attention. When she finally got her belly full of cleaning up the dog's messes, she got rid of the dog she had kept through one thing after another. Finally, I had the last straw. She brought home a dog and swore to me everything would be fine. Supposedly the dog was trained, and she promised me there'd be no problems. The dog was a beautiful dog, but was sick with distemper and not trained. He was nothing but a problem. We kept the dog confined to our kitchen. What a mess every day! The dog would have fits and literally be bouncing off the walls. The poor creature was always having seizures. When he wasn't, he would tear the place apart. He chewed all the table legs and chairs, the door moldings', and tore up the flooring until he got down to the original inlaid from when the house was built in 1923

I found myself holding this poor thing in the wee hours of the morning one night as it slipped into a coma. I sat on the kitchen floor holding, rocking, and stroking the poor animal. As I gazed up at the clock, seeing it said 2:30 am, I wondered how it was that everyone accused me of hating animals, yet I was the one sitting there with the dog dying in my arms, while the rest of the house slept soundly.

As Lizzie arose that morning and found me sitting on the floor with the dog still in my arms, I told her if the dog came out of this, the humane thing to do was to put it to sleep. The disease was taking its toll, and it wasn't fair to the animal to put it through hell for the sake of her not wanting to part with it. With that I trudged off to work saying to myself, "There's no rest for the weary." That evening, we put the dog down.

I was very stressed at work. The help was not showing up and my partner was doing nothing but working on his own car. I had smoke coming out of my ears. I spoke to Eddie, making my points clearly without flipping out. I told him if I were doing what he was; nothing would be getting done in the shop. "When do I get a break?" I asked him

He said nothing. He seemed to pick up his butt for a bit and then went right back to the same pattern. After five years of hard work I suggested selling the business or asked him what it would take to buy him out. He returned that question with what _I felt was a ridiculous figure. I'd be damned if I was going to make him any wealthier than he was when it was my persistence and hard work that made Mint Transmissions a success. So we agreed to put the business up for sale. Eddie's mother was in real estate. We agreed to let her handle the sale.

After many months of effort, Eddie and I were not having any luck with selling our business. We opened with the country in a recession in '83 and now the markets were crashing in '88. A lot of options were popping into my head. Then Eddie announced he was going to be moving to upstate New York. Good God, now I knew he'd have another excuse to be getting in late in the mornings and a reason to leave at three every day. That was it—my mind was made up. I told him, "Let's liquidate. I've had enough. I want to get out!" I couldn't get reliable help or rely on him. There were so many mornings where I got in at 7 am and started pushing and moving vehicles by myself. By 8 am I was wiped out already. I felt like I worked and ran a business that needed a crew and did it all by myself.

To top this all off, Lizzie's younger brother caught his wife having an affair and dragged my household into it. He was living now more in my house than his own. His problems became the overwhelming topic of discussion in my house. He was in my home with his two kids and his dog, a dog that was now destroying my beautiful newly refinished home. I begged Lizzie to keep the dog contained, but she could care less.

We started having a lot of problems with Destiny, as she was feeling neglected. Lizzie was telling me she wanted to join some group in the church parish. I told her, "Do you realize your kids are starving for your attention, especially Destiny?"

It was Destiny's last year in parochial grade school. I could see that she was yearning for her mother to spend time with and shop for a graduation dress. Destiny had gone on a school trip, and when I went to pick her up from the bus, her face was a picture of sadness that made my heart ache. No matter what I said to her I couldn't lift her spirits. I told Lizzie, I thought she shouldn't spend time in any more groups and to spend time with her children. She joined another group anyway.

The biggest blow came to Destiny when Lizzie handed her a dress for her graduation that came from Lizzie's cousin's daughter. I think Destiny was devastated. Destiny was not an easy child to raise. She was hyperactive and high strung, a real handful; she was always fighting and teasing her sisters and always in trouble of some kind. She couldn't seem to control herself. Lizzie's lack of interest towards her was starting to send her down a deeper, darker path.

She wanted her mother's attention and needed to bond with her at this point in her life. It broke Destiny's heart that her mother did not want to spend the time with her. She wanted a new dress she could call her own. It bothered her that it was a hand-me-down. I tried to settle the situation, making light of it. I assured her it was a beautiful dress and she'd look gorgeous in it. I even offered to go with her and get something new. This brought out an adamant "No." from Lizzie, and Destiny was doomed to accept it.

My home had become Lizzie's childhood home. "Dysfunctional," that was the word. All the bizarre situations of what she grew up in she managed to turn our lives into the same mess. Yes, I know these things go on in life, but to do battle every day with everyone in the household is not normal. She fought with me constantly and over what, I still don't know. I was convinced she was a miserable human being. She would even fight with herself in the mirror. I was leaving for work one morning, and as I passed the kitchen, she sat there with a cup of coffee. I greeted her with a "Good morning."

"Don't fucking talk to me. 1 haven't had my second cup yet." She was becoming more like an animal every day. I had no time to dwell on it and went about my day.

I tended to the closing of the business. My back was constantly going out on me. I was so stressed from fighting with my wife and everything else that was going on. I had to think about going back to work for someone when this was all over. I dreaded that. I had gotten used to being my own boss. I knew it would be a hard transition for me. I didn't worry about finding a job, but having to answer to someone again that knew less than I did would be the challenge.

Once again my wonderful partner informed me that he couldn't make it into the shop because he was busy packing and moving his belongings to go upstate. Nice! As usual I was left to do everything on my own, cleaning out the shop, all the heavy equipment, and transmissions. Somehow my God gave me the strength. This is not to say that I didn't hurt myself along the way. I was always exacerbating the injuries I sustained while being in the Navy. Now I was adding new ones.

As I hung from the rafters one-handed, taking transmission cores down from the top shelving, my one armed actions with all the weight I ended up tearing a disc in my upper back between my neck and shoulder blades. I had no time to whine about it and pushed myself for weeks until everything was finished. In the end I was bitter about how I felt Eddie took advantage of me. I was glad to be done with him. I let him know about it in a letter I sent him. I never saw him again.

My home was an unhappy home! I had to be strong for everyone and hold it all together. I got a job at an Aamco transmission shop a little further up into East New York. The cut in my income was going to be rough to handle. I had reached a certain plateau in life and never thought I'd drop down the ladder again. Conditions were the usual.. .not easy. I had set my shop up very professionally, because I knew what was required through experience to really make things work. Most bosses didn't care, especially ones that bought businesses with no knowledge of the trade.

Ray, my new boss, had been in the cookie making business. He had his wife, Ann, handling the office and business end. She seemed to know more than he did. One good thing was there were two other rebuilders employed beside myself. It would make for a shared work load in a busy shop. But, as time progressed, Ray saw I was able to handle just about anything. Eventually, the two other men disappeared. I was handling everything on my own again.

As I continued to carry more than my share of the work load at the shop, conditions at home worsened progressively. My wife was never happy with anything anymore. Not even the neighborhood. It was changing, I grant you, but not in such a terrible way, I thought.

She kept talking about moving to Florida. It sounded interesting to me with warm weather and all the other things you hear Florida has to offer. It would be a whole different life style. So I suggested a trip to visit her Aunt Leona, who lived in Inverness. We could get away from our routine for a while. Break our cycle of madness and even take the girls to Disney World while looking around and getting an idea of things.

We made plans and I decided when I would take my week vacation. I knew Ray, my boss, would be pulling his hair out without me there, so I started teaching him some basics in rebuilding transmissions. Gradually, I taught him how to do some of the more common units that he might see while I was away. This would ensure the business would keep up with itself until my return.

Time drew nearer to my leaving, and Ray approached me, propositioning me on my return that possibly I could extend myself to come in earlier and stay later in order to catch up on things. He also informed me that I wasn't entitled to a week's vacation pay, since I wasn't with his shop for a complete year yet.

I yessed him sarcastically and decided to take my tool box with me as I left. I already had enough of being taken advantage of. I made up my mind I would look for another job on my return from Florida. I would call work to let them know while I was down there. I wasn't in the mood for a confrontation now.

I backed my car into the shop's driveway and loaded my tool box into the vehicle. Ray ran out of the shop asking why I was taking my tool box. I replied that I had some repair work to do on my vehicle while I was home that week. That seemed to satisfy him for the moment. I started to drive out into the street when I heard a voice yelling my name. I looked back and saw Ray running towards me waving an envelope. I stopped and he approached me.

"We decided to pay you for the week. Have a good vacation."

"Oh, thank you, Ray," I said as I reached for the envelope. I knew I wasn't returning.

The next week I called him from Florida. Ann, Ray's wife, answered the phone. I said hello and asked to speak to Ray. "Ray went fishing, Bobby. What can I help you with?" I couldn't believe how he could take off and not worry about his own business after all the time I spent teaching him what to do when I was gone. He wasn't worried; he just figured I'd take care of it all when I returned. The load was always on me! I let Ann know I wouldn't be returning. She made it a point to let me know how disappointed she was in me. I, in turn, reciprocated. I was equally disappointed in her and Ray. It was time to relax and enjoy the rest of my vacation!

PURPLE PEOPLE EATER

Vacation, like all vacations, was never long enough. Our next episode would begin before this vacation would end. I sat comfortably in the air conditioned trailer home of Lizzie's Aunt Leona, who lived in Florida. I heard my daughter Eva calling me. Not quite three years old, she needed help getting off the toilet. I went in to help her and as I glanced in the toilet, I noticed blood in her stool. I checked her bottom right away to make sure she had no cuts or abrasions. She was fine. I asked her if she felt okay and she said yes. I was very concerned and discussed it with Lizzie and her aunt, who was a retired nurse.

Aunt Leona tried to assure us not to worry, that it may or may not be anything, and just to keep observing her when we arrived home in the next day or two. Watching her we weren't sure we were seeing anything but her stool appeared not to be normal.

When we got home we started noticing small purple dots appearing in different places on her body. These dots slowly were becoming larger and larger until they were not dots anymore, but patches of purple. We were in touch with her doctor who then advised that she may be having an allergic reaction to something.

Upon returning home my Eva was getting worse. We were seeing an allergist, and he was giving her medication. Even he was stumped. Eva got so bad she was purple all over and swelling up. You couldn't touch her. Her joints and her skin had become so sensitive to the touch. Now she was having loose and bloody bowel movements and had no control over herself anymore. Lizzie was spent by the time I got home, and I had all to do to gather my last bits of energy to take care of her during the night. I never dwelled on things. I just did it and got it over with. That's always been my motto. I'll do whatever has to be done no matter what. God and my daughters knew that I would be called on through this ordeal and be tested.

Eva was now losing all control. My baby was in agonizing pain. My daughter Lorrie screamed for me as Lorrie and Eva shared a standard sized bed to sleep in. I sprang from my sleep. Eva was crying. Lorrie, not knowing what to do, told me Eva had soiled the bed. I lifted Lorrie out of the bed, made a place for her to sleep on the floor, and then I lifted Eva. I held her as she lost control, all over me, the rugs and floors. Running with her to the bathroom, I held my tears back. I cleaned her and the floors, changed the sheets, and continued this scenario a number of times that evening. I placed Lorrie back in bed telling her to let me know as soon as she thinks Eva needed help. This continued day and night.

Finally, Saturday, the end of that week, Eva started to run an exceptionally high fever. We got in touch with her doctors and immediately headed for the emergency room at Brookdale Hospital. I stood there holding Eva trying not to hurt her. She was in pain and burning up. Lizzie was furious about the emergency room condition. They were checking out families like it was a regular visit to the clinic and not an emergency room.

After standing there an hour and a half, I lost it. I went over to the window where a nurse was checking vitals of a family with milk and cookies on the table talking and laughing. I started banging on the window and got the nurse's attention. "You see this?" I asked, showing my purple, swollen and on fire daughter. "This is an emergency, not that shit you are doing. I'm waiting here, you're playing, and my daughter is dying!"

I turned to Lizzie, "Let's get out of here." Everyone on line was flabbergasted. I was beside myself. I told Lizzie, "Let's just go to the hospital close to our house, Kings Highway Hospital." When we got there I told Lizzie to stay in the car with the baby. "Let me go in and talk to them first, and see what they say." I parked outside their emergency room and ran in. There was a nurse right at the front door behind the information desk. I described Eva's condition to her and what had transpired at Brookdale. The nurse practically screamed at me, "Oh my God! Get her in here right now!"

I hurried back to the car, grabbed Eva and Lizzie and ran back in the door.

The nurse already had a doctor there to look at the baby. "Geeze, she's burning up! She has purpuric wine rash. We can't handle her here. We've got to get her to Coney Island Emergency. They'll explain everything there. We have no time to waste. Do you want to take her or we'll send her in an ambulance? It will be quicker if you get her there right now. I will set everything up. Go! They'll be expecting you!" I told the doctor I would take her,

At Coney Island Emergency they were waiting just as the doctor had said. In the wheelchair she went to the special elevator and a room where they checked all her vitals. All around were deep sinks packed with ice. They gave her a shot and told us her heart was about to give out. Her heart rate and blood pressure were sky high, and they had to break her fever immediately. It was a matter of life and death. I died a thousand deaths when she screamed as they put her into the ice. We didn't understand what was wrong with her. We just knew that they had to save her. Then they could explain it all.

Eva was but minutes away from us losing her. But the doctors' and nurses feverish efforts saved my little girl's life. We were so grateful to them and to God above. As it turned out, Eva was suffering from an allergic reaction of some kind. That was all that could be determined. As to what it was, no one knew. I had suspicions, but I didn't say anything yet. After a brief stay in the hospital and as Eva stabilized, she was released. We had to administer different medications to her to get rid of what they called purpuric wine rash, which was her blood vessels bursting under the skin. When those patches were all connected, she looked like a giant black and blue mark. Her body from head to toe was purple.

We continued to see the allergist trying different medications which were more and more elaborate and expensive. The doctors explained that what we were able to see was only a fraction of what was going on inside of her. Whatever was causing what we were seeing was eating her up internally, too.

Amidst all this havoc I was constantly working in the house in whatever little spare time I had. I had so many projects going on. Everything started and nothing finished. We started calling it Bob's halfway house. Now Lorrie was preparing to make her Communion. Lizzie was pressing me to finish everything before that because she wanted to have all our family over for the festivities.

I had so much to do, I was overwhelmed. I remodeled the kitchen that I was forced to do because the dogs had done so much damage. The rest of the house still had a long way to go, and I was doing it all by myself. You have to understand, this was all major renovations from the entrance, foyer, parlor, living room, and dining room. I used to say to Lizzie, "Do you dream this stuff during the night?" She would tell me close these windows up, knock this wall down, put a window here, French doors there, new banister going up to the second floor, and strip the stairs back to the natural wood. It was so much, yet I always wanted to please and be accommodating. I did everything she asked for. I literally worked around the clock, sometimes, going to bed at four in the morning, then getting up again at seven am and heading to the shop. I was exhausted, but I did finish everything in time.

Lorrie's Communion turned out beautiful, and everyone loved the place. I don't know if Lizzie was happy or not. Nothing ever seemed to make her happy. Basically, she did things because she felt she had to, not because she enjoyed it. It all took a toll on me though.

The following week after the party, I collapsed going up the stairs after having come home from work. I lay on the steps with spasms and in pain and yelled to Lizzie to call an ambulance, because I couldn't move and I didn't know what was wrong with me. She decided to wait—the one that was always in a rush to go to the doctors! She thought if I lay in a hot tub of water it would help all the spasms. Somehow I managed to crawl up the stairs and drag myself over the edge of the tub. I told her to throw some Epson salts in. I swore I was having Charlie horses running through my stomach into my back.

I lay there in the hot water for about two hours until I started to feel a little relief.

I made it to the bedroom and fell into a sleep that felt like I was out for two days straight. I learned a lesson: No matter how strong you think you are, you can only do so much without getting any rest or sleep. You pay consequences for whatever you do in life

Eva's condition gradually grew worse. Her bowel movements became more frequent, more loose and bloody. The doctors couldn't figure out what was wrong with her. We went from one therapy to another. Eventually we were recommended by the allergist to see a specialist in internal medicine. He was based in Brookdale Hospital. I wasn't crazy about going back to Brookdale, but I was willing to do anything that would help my baby.

In addition to Eva's problem we had all kinds of added turmoil in the house. Destiny's behavior was always out of control and so was Lizzie's. She was arguing with me over I don't know what. Each day

I came home from work, said hello, all I got was dirty looks, which was a constant.

I looked at Destiny with disdain and fear, "What did I do now?" Destiny just shrugged her shoulders.

Of course, Lizzie finally chimed in. "If you don't know, I'm not telling you!"

I just shook my head and walked away. I was starting to realize that whatever was going on in life, good, bad or indifferent--was going to be my fault. We needed a fall guy, someone to blame everything on. I was it.

HELL HOUSE

Poor little Eva was going through hell! We met with the specialist at Brookdale Hospital. More test, more therapies. What this little girl didn't go through! it was breaking my heart. I was worried sick over her. Lizzie was at her wits end. I kept saying that I had a feeling it had something to do with all the medicines she had been given for strep throat, but no one would listen to me. The doctor didn't agree with me. He was looking for something else. I don't think he even knew what he was looking for. But you know doctors ... they'll never admit to you that they're baffled. They'll just keep running tests.

Lizzie had an inkling that maybe I was right in my connection of the narcotics that were given to Eva for strep throat and her allergic reaction. After spending a week in the medical section of the library we found a toxin linked to an overdose of drugs that could cause all this damage. In speaking with the doctor, I asked him if in all his testing, he had tested for C Difficle toxin, He told me no, and that it was far-fetched. He was positive that wasn't Eva's problem. I said, "You know what doc, I want you to do this test, I don't care what the cost is, I don't care what you think. We are all exhausted here and Eva is getting more and more ill. We are around the clock with her on the toilet bleeding and sick!"

I was very upset and wouldn't relent until he agreed. We would keep the medical regiment that Eva was on until we received results and we would go from there.

I finally came home one day and asked Lizzie if she ever heard from the doctor or if she had called to find out any results. She said no. I asked her what she was waiting for? Eva couldn't go on like this.

"I can't go on like this either," was Lizzie's reply. "I know something is going on with you at work with that new secretary your boss hired!"

I stared, dumbfounded, "Are you serious? I'm working in a shop with 22 men. I work on one side of the building in the back, and she's upstairs on the other side in the boss's office. What, am I screwing her under the lifts?"

"Do you say hello to her?"

"Well, yeah, but so what? Everyone says hello, good morning."

Lizzie held film, "You're not here for me anymore. I don't feel it."

I told her if she was not feeling it, it was her, not me. She accused me of not helping her, that I was "somewhere else."

"Are you crazy? Who do you think is doing things every night, little elves? I'm NOT screwing around! Give me the doctor's number and let me call him. I'll bet Eva tested positive and that is why he hasn't called. He's ashamed to tell me the results and give in to the fact that we were right."

I called the doctor and sure enough, he said, "Oh yes, yes. I'm sorry; I meant to get back to you. The results are positive."

Now we finally knew where we were heading and how to treat Eva. The "c deficile" toxin was eating Eva's insides. Now the question was could we get it under control and how much damage had been done?

We had to go to a pharmacy on Long Island. They were the only ones that carried the particular drug that could help Eva. When we got there the pharmacist told me I'd better sit down. I didn't. "Just tell me the price."

The cost of this medication knocked us for a loop. We couldn't afford it. My brother-in-law Joe and my sister MaryAnn paid for it. Thank God for their help, otherwise, I don't know what we would have done. It was a liquid with exactly a ten-day supply. It was like gold. Every time Eva would spit it out, I would suck it back off the table with an eyedropper. We had to get it down her at all costs and then use another medication indefinitely. This one was a powder, and I learned to disguise it in chocolate syrup to get her to swallow it.

We reached a point where Eva's symptoms were controlled, but she was not getting better. Too much damage had been done. Through all of this, Lizzie had finally and completely, totally lost her mind. She fought with me day and night, accusing me of affairs and anything else that was wrong in life. She wanted to move to Florida to start a new life. I suggested she see a doctor. She did and was supposed to be on medication to control whatever anxiety and anything else she was experiencing.

She went to see a psychologist and insisted I also go see him. I went just so there wouldn't be more to fight about. I was sick all the time. I couldn't sleep. I was afraid, sometimes she'd attack me during the night, hitting me, swinging wildly with her fist. She'd leave me lengthy letters that she would insist I read before I left for work at 7 am. My eyes were blood shot and hurting from migraine headaches I was experiencing from all the stress. My back was going out constantly. I got to the psychologist one evening bent over and I could hardly move or walk. As he opened the door to let me in, he said, "Oh my God! Does she fight with you even when you're like this?"

"Yes," I admitted, "even as I'm on my hands and knees, crawling across the floor."

Nothing changed with all the therapy and counseling she was getting except that I was going broke paying for it. Of course, her relating to misguided friends, her warped perception of things, only fueled the fires with their advice to her. I started referring to my home as Hell House. I didn't even want to walk in the door after work. I would always take a deep breath and sigh as I never knew what I was about to walk into. Sometimes, I would go into work in the mornings and get myself set, when the shop phone would begin to ring at 8 am. They'd call me, "Bobby, it's for you."

I'd answer hello, not able to imagine who would be calling me at work so early in the morning. It was Lizzie. I'd hear her spew, "Fuck you, Bobby, fuck you! You hear me? Fuck you!" I'd hang up. She was nuts.

With Eva finally stabilizing a little, the rest of the dysfunction in my home continued. We put the house up for sale. Lizzie kept telling me she was going to make a trip down to Florida ahead of time in order to set everything up. She'd stay with her aunt in Inverness, find a house to rent, and set up the kids for school.

Everything is easier said than done. I knew it was never going to happen. I went along with whatever she said. I had enough on my plate to worry about and take care of. I knew that when the time came, I'd be the one to make everything happen and go smoothly.

Fighting and arguing escalated with Lizzie becoming more and more physical. I was standing at the kitchen sink rinsing my hands. My back was toward her as she yelled at me with my never knowing what she was yelling about. Suddenly, I felt a knee into the small of my back as she leaped at me. I buckled at the sink in pain. It seemed she wasn't happy until she saw me miserable.

Another incident when we were in the kitchen yelling at each, she shoved me hard against the doorway molding leading into our half bath off the kitchen. I had double vision for the next two days after my head slammed and bounced off the molding. She was physically attacking me all the time now. I was afraid to sleep at night, as she would run from the downstairs kitchen, where she was working herself into frenzy, yelling and crying to herself in the middle of the night, disturbing the kids. When she worked herself up enough she'd charge up the stairs, swinging wildly with her fist as I lie in the bed. I jumped up one time, finally slapping her in the face, shocking her back to reality.

She'd run back out of the room, grumbling about how I didn't love her. She was right! She was drawing the life out of me.

I felt badly and guilty that I struck her, but I was starting to fear for my life.

She'd come up sometimes with a kitchen knife in her hand. She even charged at me with the baseball bat I had for our protection beside the bed.

I can't say I was an angel through all this, but she was bringing out the worst in me. Lizzie used to call sometimes before I left work to tell me to stop and pick up things at the store before I got home. I never understood that. She'd sit home all day with the car in the driveway and I was the one that had to go shopping after work.

One Friday evening she called me at work and said, "Let's have pizza tonight." No problem. I never expected her to cook every night of the week, and we often took breaks from the routine. "After you order the pie, go across to the little superette and pick up these things for me," and she'd give me her list. It was Friday, and the whole neighborhood seemed to have the same idea.

I pulled up to the pizza parlor. There were no parking spots anywhere, not even for double parking. This is Brooklyn; it's congested. I finally found a spot, ran into the pizza place which was so mobbed, you could hardly walk in. I yelled my order and told the guy I'd be back. I went across the street for some groceries. Again, there was a long line to check out. I got back to the parlor and still the pie wasn't done. God knows how many people were ahead of me with pies still in the oven cooking.

Ah, finally, I'm out of there and on the way home. I pulled into the driveway as close to the side door as I could so I didn't have to walk too far. I manage to wriggle my way in through the side door with a bag of groceries in one hand and balanced the burning hot pizza pie in the other. I got in the door, looked up, and was greeted with, "Where the fuck were you? We're all starving."

I explained, "It's Friday night and the places are all packed."

"Yeah, yeah, yeah, everything is a fucking problem," she said as she grabbed the grocery bag from my hand. "You're nothing but a guinea bastard!"

With that, I snapped. I was exhausted from work and then I was running around like a mad man. I let her have it. "Why couldn't you call the pizza place ahead of time if you were in such a hurry? I could have just stopped in, picked it up, and then done the grocery shopping. You're home all day!"

With fury in her eyes, she told me, "Fuck you, fuck you, fuck you, just give me the pie!"

"You want the pie?" I asked, as I opened up the side door and threw it out into the alley.

"There's your fucking pie!"

I left and went out for Chinese food. I didn't know what they did for dinner and I didn't care, I was so exhausted and upset.

My life with Lizzie had become an endless nightmare. It was the weekend now. God only knew what I would be in for. It was Saturday and the girls were in the yard playing. I was in the kitchen watching them out the back window, when Lizzie crept up on me, muttering again about my having an affair with the boss's secretary. The only place I was having an affair was in her mind. I never cheated, not even with all she had been putting me through. I always gave the same respect I wanted in a relationship.

My thoughts were interrupted with a blaze of her wildly swinging fist. She was screaming, "1 hate you, I hate you!" She was in an off-the-wall frenzy and rage and taking it out on me. I put my arms up to defend myself. With all the black and blues she got from hitting me, I knew she told her friends I was beating her. This episode got so frenzied that she slipped and fell right on her tailbone. I looked down on her with disgust. I felt nothing for her. I didn't help her, not even as she was yelling out in agony. I couldn't believe my own reaction as I walked away feeling nothing. Nothing, not feeling bad she hurt herself or feeling anything about what she said to me or called me. I was like an empty shell... and I knew once again I would be out eating Chinese food. It was becoming a staple for me.

The following days and weeks were nothing but insanity. In between the bouts of yelling, screaming, and fighting, there was nothing but tension, stress, and coldness in the house. You could cut it with a knife, it was so thick. I was very concerned for Eva. With every episode that went on, Eva's problems would flare. I even begged Lizzie to stop for Eva's sake. My little girl was so sick. It all seemed to fall on deaf ears.

I came home one evening to find all my things in bags at the side steps leading out to the door. I came in and, mystified, said, "What the. . ?"

"Get out; you don't love me, go with your girlfriend!" Oh, here we go again, I thought.

"That's right, you fucking bastard!" she screamed as she ran down the stairs swinging at me. I started to pick my things up and opened the door to exit.

I heard a hysterical shout. "Nooooo, don't leave me!" she said as she grabbed me and was wrestling the bags out of my hands.

"I've got to get out of here." I dropped my belongings. I couldn't take another minute. As I tried to leave she tore at my clothing, tearing my jacket and pulling the shirt off my back, I went out the door into the cold air with just my slacks on. I cried to myself. I couldn't take much more.

I sat in my car freezing, waiting for the heater to work. I was getting hungry. I was a nervous eater. I had to eat when I was upset to my stomach, just to ease the pain in my gut. Of course it was into a Chinese take-out somewhere with no clothes on. I was getting all kinds of wild looks as I entered the take-out.

I got back into the car looking for a spot I could pull over to eat. I found an out-of-the-way spot that seemed serene, opened the bag only to find that they forgot to give me utensils to eat with. What was I going to do now? It was the kind of dish that was definitely not a finger food. I had a thought. I was near my parents' house, and they weren't home. I could go in without any questions and get a fork. I headed over, pulled into their driveway and went to the front door with my keys.

Rummaging through my pockets I thought, "What the hell? Don't tell me I don't have my house keys." I spotted something and was relieved. "This is the key." I got the door open, but my dad has another lock from the inside with a chain. This key I didn't have. I sat back in the car, so hungry, so distraught.

What was I going to do? I was starved, so I decided I'd drink the food down until I remembered I had a pocket knife in the glove compartment. I attempted the knife as a utensil, but wound up slicing my mouth open from the inside out. I began to bleed all over myself and into what was left of my food and down my chin onto my chest. I was so distraught; I began to feel sorry for myself and cried.

Why does my life have to be like this, why dear God? I thought. I'm still being punished for the one bad thing I did in my entire life. My conscience was haunting me about not returning the wallet I found when I was in the service.

In between all this tumult we were showing the house to potential buyers. Thank God we finally got a buyer. This was just added stress that Lizzie couldn't handle. For me it was no big deal. I tried to reassure Lizzie that when it sells, it sells. Why blow things up bigger than what they have to be, overwhelming yourself?

Getting home from a hard day at work I was able to get a parking spot in front of the house. I parked my car and walked up the driveway. I could see there was something attached to the side door window and wondered what it was. My question was answered as I got to the door. It was a note from Lizzie. I took a deep breath and said, "What now?" Reading to myself, "Welcome home! I prepared an evening for the two of us. The kids are taken care of and spending the night at their girlfriends' pajama parties. I prepared a bath for you and laid out your suit on the bed. Then we'll have a special dinner together in the dining room. We'll spend time alone and have a wonderful evening."

Oh God! I took a deep breath and knew I was about to enter Hell House again! Prepared my bath? Laid out my shirt? It was a weeknight after work. What did she think we're doing, living in a soap opera? I walked in, glanced up the foyer steps leading to the kitchen, and there she was—standing there dressed in a dark blue gown, like she was going to a wedding. I didn't say a word. I was afraid to. She told me to go upstairs, bathe, and get dressed. She'd be waiting for me in the living room. I walked through the dining room, past the table and saw it was set with our best china and candles, very elegantly. I'm thinking, "Oh God, she is really off the wall!"

We had been fighting for weeks. She had hated me in the morning when I left. Now it was as if someone had flipped a switch. It was like someone else was there. I bathed, got dressed in my suit and tie, afraid to not go along with her fantasy.

I walked into the living room and sat down beside her on the couch. Lizzie handed me a glass of wine and said, "Isn't this nice to sit here together?" We continued to make small talk. Then she started asking me meaningless questions about how I felt towards certain things and our future together. I was starting to tense up because I could feel her leading in a direction that was going to be trouble. I knew she had things on her mind that she was going to pursue.

And then it came out. "And about that Linda! I know there's something going on between you and your boss's secretary. Come on, tell me the truth, stop lying."

"Why do you even go there?" I asked. "I keep telling you there's nothing going on. You have to stop imagining things in your mind."

"You're a fucking liar!" she shouted as she started to hit me with her fists. "I hate you, I hate you, I hate you! You fucking guinea bastard!" Ranting and raving, carrying on like a crazed lunatic; she became increasingly agitated and hysterically insane. She screamed and cursed at me every foul word you could think of. She finally started to wear herself out as I said nothing and added no fuel to the fire. I was getting sicker inside with every passing moment. She finally ran upstairs crying loudly her phony cries.

I shuffled into the dining room, blew out the candles, and sat at the long, long table eating dinner alone. I listened to her rants from above me as I tried to ingest food to settle my nervous stomach, praying that this would end soon. But it was only the beginning.

Lizzie started to run up and down the stairs more frantically, screaming her curses at me. Looking up from my plate, I said, "Enough already!" But anything I said seemed to spur her on more feverishly,

"Enough! Nothing's enough! You fuck! I'll kill you, you no good bastard!" I bolted from the table as she lunged for me.

"I can't even eat in peace," I muttered.

"Peace? I'm going to cut you into pieces!" She ran into the kitchen. I heard her going through the cutlery draw. I bolted up the steps, ran into the bedroom, and rushed out of my suit. I threw on jeans and a T-shirt, as I heard a crack as she burst through the bedroom louver doors that had beautiful blue Plexiglas inserts. I ran around to the other side of the bed. She was flailing her arms, swinging the carving knife she held in her hand yelling and cursing at me. She ran around the bed attacking me. I jumped onto and over the bed to get away from her and exited the bedroom. I stood still for a moment on the broken shards of blue glass, watching her as she started to break things in our bedroom.

She finally kicked through the legs on a beautiful Chippendale table I had professionally restored. The table fell over, and our wedding picture that sat in a very ornate gold frame scratched grooves into the inlaid top as it hit the floor. Glass splintered through the photo and across the floor. How befitting, I thought. My heart was breaking along with everything else. I yelled at her, "You have absolutely no regard for anything."

I had the feeling this was going to be an endless night. I decided to go and back my car up across our driveway. Lizzie had a habit of driving off angrily in our Chrysler after working herself up over something. I knew if she left tonight she would end up hurting herself or killing someone else.

I came back into the house to endless outbursts of craziness. At 2 am she did just as I suspected and rushed into our 5th Avenue Chrysler. I wondered where she thought she would go with my shop car blocking the driveway. This infuriated her even more. She was determined to leave. She violently made K-turn maneuvers from the driveway onto our front lawn, destroying all the landscape, shrubs, and sod, finally wedging the car sideways in between the front stoop and our neighbor's front yard fence. She got out of the car, furious and spewing curse words. One of the neighbors was walking his dog and commented to her that he didn't think she'd get out of there. She responded to his shock with a quick "Fuck you"

Upon her return into the house she continued her lunacy through the early morning hours. I lay down in my bed afraid of closing my eyes as she continued to run up and down from the first floor, attacking me with her fist. It was soon day light. Like a sleepless zombie I ran past her as she screamed profanities at me. On my way to work I thanked the Lord for watching over me during the night!

I knew after this incident I couldn't go on like this anymore. I was becoming incoherently senseless and an animal just like she was. I was a firecracker always ready to explode. Whenever I was home it was constant battling over nothing. After Lizzie's insistent badgering for hours, my patience would wear. I'd flip out blasting her at the top of my lungs. She would run around to all the windows in the house slamming them shut, yelling, "The neighbors, the neighbors!" She'd have me so bent I didn't care about anything or anyone anymore. I'd go to the window and open wide and scream out "fuck the neighbors!" She turned me into a mad man.

We continued this dysfunctional relationship for what seemed an endless period of time. The closing date for the sale of our house was set. It was time for the big move to Florida. Lizzie never did manage to drive down and set anything up like she said she would. Now we had the added stress of a major move. I was drained but I kept pushing myself. My back was out constantly. All my other injuries were exacerbated by all the stress. I was in serious pain. I was having a hard time walking, standing, and doing just about anything.

I started to wonder deep in thought. I felt like I was dead, not just physically, but emotionally. I didn't want to be with her anymore, As much as I loved my kids, I realized this household had become completely dysfunctional. It was not good for the girls' health or their best interest that this lifestyle continued. What does it mean when you say your marriage vows, till death do you part? Did it mean just physically or emotionally as well? I thought about this and everything that would result if I made a decision to separate from Lizzie. I pondered this deeply, realizing also that I was not myself any longer. I was sick, emotionally dead and distraught and no good to myself or anyone else.

I waited for what seemed like the right moment to break the news to Lizzie. She was starting to speak to me about the move and that's when I told her. "I have something to tell you. I've decided not to make the move with you down to Florida. It is not good for the girls to continue this way. The move to Florida was intended to be for a better life. I don't see it happening. We have a lot of problems. All we're going to do is move them from one place to another. I'm sorry but this is best for everyone."

Lizzie responded, lovingly hugged me and said. "You don't mean that! I love you!" I wanted to vomit. I stood there with my arms down, stone cold like a statue. I couldn't even look at her. My gaze was right at her but through her. I saw nothing and felt nothing. She began to beg and plead with me not to do this, to please come with her and the girls. I kept repeating, "I'm sorry, I can't do this."

It wasn't long before her horns emerged again. I started walking away and her demeanor changed. She once again yelled and cursed, "You fucking bastard! I want my share of the house in a check to me at closing!"

"Fine," I responded, "Make sure you tell the lawyer."

The day of the closing came and went. She got her share as she wanted. I didn't know how she and my girls were getting to Florida and I didn't care. She told me nothing. I only knew the date we were to be out of the house. Lizzie finally told me they'd be moving and staying with her aunt ahead of time so she could locate a house to rent. The moving company wouldn't be down for at least a week after picking up our belongings. I took nothing; I kept only my clothing and my records. Lizzie ended up leaving after the movers came. It broke my heart to say goodbye to Destiny, Lorrie, and Eva. I told them I would always love them and we would stay in touch by phone and letters.

I told them, "Please don't be upset. Things will be better without me in the house for your mother to fight with. Don't worry, everything will work out. I love you!" I hugged and kissed them, trying not to cry. I needed to stay strong to show them there was no need to be upset.

A TIME TO CONTEMPLATE

I was emotionally drained. The house was now eerily empty and strangely hushed. I had a few days before I had to leave. I opened a fold up bed and slept in Lorrie and Eva's bedroom. I didn't want to go back in my own room. For some reason, it just made me sick. Too many bad memories I guess.

I didn't think I would sleep, but exhaustion took over. I awoke to sunlight shining through the bedroom window. I could hear the birds singing. It was a beautiful morning, very calm and peaceful. This was all I ever wanted, to simply have peace and harmony in my life. I realized that nothing else mattered. Peace was all I cared about.

I decided to quit working. I was a mess. I had forgotten to think about what I was going to do and where I'd go. My folks insisted that I stay with them until I felt better when I could think clearly. I put the money from the sale of the house in the bank and didn't touch it. I really didn't know what I was going to do. My dad kept telling me I needed some time to heal, and so I didn't pursue anything legally for a divorce. I decided to give that time also.

I slept in my sister's old bedroom. I couldn't walk in the mornings. I crawled across the floor from my sister's old room to the bathroom; hoist myself up, pulling myself by holding onto the towel bar. Slowly, I'd try to take care of my personal needs and get dressed. I couldn't turn my head to the left for a few months. The stress had made me knotted up so terribly that I was in pain with every move I made. I would try to take walks after lunch or dinner managing only to go a few house length, turn and make my way back.

I'd hold onto people's fences to prevent myself from losing my balance due to the weakness I felt while standing. With each day I would walk a little further until I was able to walk two blocks and get to church on Sunday. St. Edmund's was only a short walk from the house. I prayed so intently to God to heal me and for the Angels to watch over my girls.

It was the summer of 1989. Lizzie had been corresponding with me since she and the girls got settled in the house she rented. All the letters were very loving, telling me she wanted me back. The main thing was that the girls missed me, and I missed them. With that, I made the decision to go and visit.

I was so happy to see my daughter's, I stayed a week and of course during that time even the girls worked on convincing me to come back. Lizzie seemed calm. She promised the world that things would be different if I returned. I left and felt empty leaving my children again. It's so hard to separate from family and ties you have after 18 years of knowing someone.

I went back to Brooklyn, confused and torn. Maybe the separation was good. I thought that maybe it brought Lizzie back to reality. Maybe things could change. I missed my daughters so much.

Like a fool I made the choice to rejoin the family. I packed my 57 Chevy with my belongings and loaded them onto a train in Virginia as I headed down to Florida

Things seemed to stay calm for a while. We were busy. Eva started to have major flare ups with her medical condition. So we were between hospitals and doctors again. In the meantime we wanted a house of our own.

I, as usual, was eager to please everyone. We looked in subdivisions outside the city of Orlando. We found property right on a lake and decided to build a house. I was hesitant to take my proceeds from my Brooklyn sale and use them towards the new purchase. But, I figured if we spent less than the cost of a house in Brooklyn we would be left with a cushion in the bank. We'd have a home paid out right, lower bills, less stress, and I could work a little easier with a job not putting in so many hours.

This was not to be. Lizzie insisted on every amenity. ... She had to have the built in pool too, and couldn't wait until we had extra money. So here we go with another mortgage and the same way of life all over again. There was just no getting ahead.

Lizzie and I returned quickly to our former relationship, with her fighting with me day and night. I realized that life was about perception, of how we perceive and are perceived. We would get a lot of notes from people just trying to be nice. Lizzie would read these cards and become angry. The caption on the card might say "HI! How are you doing?" But she'd interpret it negatively. "How the fuck do they think we're doing?" with her anger directed at the sender. It amazed me how someone could say hello, and she'd say fuck you!

Eva was finally admitted to Shands Hospital in Jacksonville. We had a two hour drive to and from home. It was tiring. They didn't know what was wrong with her. As many times as I explained and gave them her history, it was like talking to the wall.

They wanted to run all kinds of tests. The day came with a new diagnosis and plan for treatment.

Now back at home Destiny's out of control behavior had Lizzie at her wit's end. She insisted on putting Destiny in a facility for troubled girls. Destiny was a mess. No one could understand things she was doing or why she was doing them. She would go out her bedroom window in the middle of the night. At 2 or 3 AM I would get up and check the girls and the entire house. Destiny was nowhere to be found. I would see her window ajar and the front door still locked from the inside. I knew she was up to no good with her teenage friends, but I realized it was all part of growing up

I confronted her and asked her one day, "Why don't you just walk out the front door?" She shrugged her shoulders and said she didn't know. I explained the ills of doing this and how we worry. It didn't seem to change much. She finally took off one night and disappeared for two weeks. Her mother and she had battled constantly. We never heard from her. I hunted through the neighborhoods on my own and finally found out she was staying at a friend's house. The mother was an idiot also for not notifying us. A friend of Destiny elaborated that she told these people she was being abused.

When Destiny finally returned, she was placed in a facility. She would have to spend six weeks there before being released. We spent our time visiting two different children in two different locations. In between that, Lizzie was fighting with me constantly. Nothing had changed. We were on a path of destruction. My Lorrie was the only one that was stable but who knows what all of this turmoil was doing to her emotionally.

Shands Hospital was in Jacksonville, two hours north of where we were living. Destiny was in another direction and a half hour or so away. But, they weren't really allowing us to visit with her. They felt this was best after a few consultations with us. The trip up north was knocking us out. Eventually Destiny came home and was worse than ever. Besides the fighting she did with her mother she would lock herself in her room and stay constantly in the dark. I was starting to see a similarity here to a few other people on Lizzie's side of the family. Depression, mood swings, euphoria one minute and down in the dumps the next.

It all made no sense at the time. I tried numerous times to have little talks with Destiny to find out what was troubling her. I tried to guide her with words in a better direction. You could never make progress. As parents, Lizzie and I were not in a united front. Lizzie was always trying to make me look like the bad guy in front of the kids. Everything was my fault. She continued to ride Destiny's back, even though I told her to give the kid some space. I think a big part of Destiny's problem was that she wanted her mother's attention, but not in this way. She was longing for that mother-daughter relationship you always hear about, almost like two sisters.

Destiny started showing suicidal tendencies. Before anything happened we had to protect her from hurting herself. Now we admitted Destiny into Shands Hospital also. I have Eva sick on one floor and Destiny in the psych ward on another floor. We traveled back and forth every day to the hospital. It felt like we were spending our lives there. Many times we were too exhausted to make the trip back home in the evenings, in the dark, so we slept on chairs in some of the hospital's waiting rooms. Finally, social workers set us up at a local Ronald McDonald house.

I was at the end of my rope, watching the doctors' experiment with Eva. I ended up having words with them. They didn't like what I had to say and basically told me to take Eva out of the hospital if I wasn't happy. I told them that were my intentions, before they killed her

After much searching, we found doctors who were experts in the field and were transferring her to a hospital in Orlando nearby where we would be living. We had complete confidence in the doctors there. We told them straight out it would be a matter of saving Eva's life. Her internal organs were destroyed from the toxins that were going through her. The damage was done and could not be reversed. They were going to do what they called a "first". They would remove almost all her colon and do a procedure called "a pull through," bringing down the small intestine into her anus. She would temporarily have a bag on the side of her stomach until the healing process was through. What a horror my poor baby was going through!

There was so much going on. Our house was completed and ready to move into. It was gorgeous but a long way from becoming a home. With boxes stacked all over, there was a lot of work to do. Lizzie continued to fight with me on a daily basis, all day and every day. I suggested that we needed help. She couldn't handle things. So she called my folks and asked them to come down and stay with us for a while.

That same weekend Eva was released so that she could visit and see her new home. My mom and dad arrived shortly after coming into the house with Eva. As everyone walked through the new house oohing and aahing, mom turned to Eva and asked "So how do you like your new house?"

Lizzie became livid and made sure I heard about it. When we were in private she said, "That bitch, I wanted to ask Eva that!"

"You're angry about that? What's the big deal? You didn't expect a grandmother to ask a grandchild a question like that?" I tried to reason. But Lizzie went on and on, pissed off as always. I realized that whenever Lizzie had anything fantasized in her mind a specific way; there was a problem if things didn't go the way she imagined.

My folks stayed in the house and took care of Lorrie and anything else that needed to be done, as we trekked to the hospital every day. Lizzie fought with me continually over everything and anything including my parents, the kids, and me! None of it made any sense and none of it mattered. She'd say something one minute, screaming it at me; I would respond and then she would tell me she never said that.

She started talking about relatives who were visiting her and telling her things. "I saw Uncle John last night and he told me... "Uncle John was dead along with the rest of her cast of characters. She was starting to show signs of multiple personalities. I thought I was talking to someone different every time we spoke.

During the following week while at Eva's bedside with Lizzie visiting her in her hospital room, I was surprised as my mother and father walked in. As they entered the room Lizzie turned and walked out, passing them without saying a word. I knew something was wrong right away. My mom waved a piece of paper with a note on it, telling me "we're leaving! " "What!" I exclaimed, confused. My mother explained they woke up to find this nasty letter on the kitchen table in the morning.

My dad looked at me and said "she's throwing us out! " I started to read the letter. I couldn't believe it! She had only just called and asked them to make the trip down to help us. Now she was telling them to leave after only a week. The situation was becoming more insane every day. I apologize to mom and dad, thanking them for all they did, knowing how much they put themselves out to come down to Florida. I assured them that I would be soon to follow. "I'm right behind you, if I last another week it will be a miracle."

We kissed and hugged as they left. I became teary-eyed. I was so emotionally shot again. When Lizzie returned .1 asked why she did that. She started fighting with me right in the hospital room "I don't want them in my house!,,

"Why did you ask them to come down?" I pleaded.

Eva, in her hospital bed, was getting upset and yelled, "Stop fighting!" I knew all this fighting was a detriment to Eva's health. We were only exacerbating her problems. Lizzie didn't seem to care about Eva's health, the well-being of the kids or the family in general, and definitely not about me. She seemed to only care about what she thought was good for her. I wondered about that. My thoughts were being fueled towards leaving permanently. I kept saying to myself, let's see what happens. I always gave people more chances than they deserved.

96 TEARS

The following weekend Destiny was allowed to come home from Shands Hospital for a visit. Perfect timing, for that Sunday was Mother's Day! Lizzie and I left for the two hour trip before noon that Friday. We had arranged to get Destiny released early so we could also go and pick up Eva at Orlando Hospital. We went up to Eva's room. Destiny helped Eva get dressed to leave, while Lizzie and I had some paper work to tend to with the hospital staff.

After we finished Lizzie started arguing with me in the hallway. She was getting louder and I kept shushing her. I saw an exit door, opened it, and led her out into a beautiful garden courtyard the hospital had for patients and visitors. She started yelling at me at the top of her lungs. She didn't care where she was accusing me of things that have happened in the past and things that had nothing to do with me. I responded to her and she told me "I never said that! " "Lizzie you just told me that, not two minutes ago. You're so enraged about I don't know what, you don't even know what you're saying anymore. You want something to get mad at? How about this: I've been holding in the fact that my baby is in the hospital because of you!" "Me?!" she said, stunned.

"That's right, I was never going to say anything, because I didn't want to make you feel bad, but I don't care anymore what you think. That's right. You could never listen to me. I was cheap, you said! You had to keep taking Eva to the doctors against my wishes. I gave in just not to fight with you and let you have your way. That's right, it's your fault.

"Kids get sick and get over it as quickly as they fall ill. My mother never took us to the doctor for every little sniffle. She used her instincts—something you don't have! Eva is lucky to be alive right now. No thanks to you. The doctors said her case is that severe that there's still a chance we might lose her. You don't even care that she gets sicker every time you are yelling and screaming in front of her." It was as if my diatribe was fading into thin air. She didn't get anything I said. It all just went over her head.

She screamed back at me "1 know you're leaving. My uncle John told me!" Whoa, here we go again, the visiting dead uncle. He told her enough.

"Call up to the floor and get Destiny." I told Lizzie. I remained in the Courtyard. I needed to calm down. I didn't even want to walk back into the hospital with her. I was embarrassed.

I stood there waiting and was approached by one of Eva's doctors. We were discussing procedures for rehabilitation, so long as the surgery was a success. Destiny suddenly approached me and asked for the car keys as her mother had accidentally locked hers in the car. Without question I handed them to her and said "tell your mother I'll be right there." I just wanted to finish speaking with the doctor.

My conversation was longer than I expected and Destiny returned with my keys and told me they were ready to go. I excused myself from the doctor. I turned and started walking with Destiny, glancing down at my keys still in my hand. I noticed right away something was not right.

"Oh how nice, your mother is a piece of work, my safety deposit key is missing!" Destiny gave me a smirk. She knew her mother stole the key, and I knew exactly what she had planned to do with it. I got in the car as she was behind the wheel. I never said another word all the way home.

That evening I started to read a bedtime story to Eva. In the middle of the peace and tranquility of the story, Lizzie charged in and shouted "I know you're leaving, you bastard! I hate you!"

I stopped reading. Eva and I looked up at her. I said, "What are you talking about?"

She started ranting about how I had all the moving boxes separated in the garage. "So what, I just organized so we know who's stuff is where and in what room things are going in.

Please, give me a break"! I was exasperated with her.

She continued yelling that I was no good and a liar. Eva piped in "ooooh please, stop fighting!"

I told Lizzie she was able to ruin anything, even a bedtime story and my trying to keep the household calm and quiet for Eva. I had even been looking forward to this weekend. It would be the first time I'd be showering and sleeping in the new house. I had been staying at the hospital continually night after night.

Saturday evening fell- I felt nothing but tension in the house since the moment we set foot in the door. I made sure I had a gift and Mother's Day card ready to give Lizzie for Sunday morning. I didn't want to give her any reason to fight with me even though special occasions had become meaningless to me.

I awoke Sunday morning in bed alone. I was thankful. Lizzie had slept in the living room. I guess she hated me so much she couldn't stomach the thought of sleeping next to me. I was barely out of bed when she charged into the room, with all the same accusations of leaving and name-calling and any other foul things she could say to me. "Happy Mother's Day," I thought to myself.

One day was the same as the next to her, it didn't matter. I had enough. I cleaned up, got dressed and took my two oldest daughters outside to speak to them. Lorrie was 11 and Destiny, 15 years of age. I thought they were old enough to understand what I was about to say to them and old enough to make a decision. They were well aware of the situation in the household. I told them what was going on was not normal and not good for their wellbeing and certainly not good for Eva's health. I told them that I wanted them to really think about what I was about to say and ask them.

I was very sick from the situation, but they were my main concern. "If you feel you can't live without me being here for you then I will do whatever it takes, whatever sacrifices necessary to be here for you girls until you are old enough to be on your own." I told them.

I believed it was in everybody's best interest for me not to be there. "Your mom won't have someone to fight with, and things will hopefully calm down. Just tell me what you think and what you want me to do."

Without hesitation both of them said, "No, daddy, don't stay, it's best to leave."

I asked each of them a number of times "Are you sure?" They reassured me that they understood everything completely and it was best for them and Eva. They were even concerned for Eva. We promised to always stay in touch with each other, and that we loved one another. We would always be a family. I would always be their daddy. This was the most heartbreaking moment of my life.

I kissed and hugged them both and told Destiny not to say anything, but to get ready to go back to the hospital. I knew it wasn't fair for her to go back early, but we had no choice. I'd drop her off on my way back to New York. I went to Eva's bedroom and spoke to her, explaining everything. She seemed to take it very well for a six-year old. I don't know what she was really thinking or understanding. I just felt it was good that the girls were staying calm.

I gathered my clothes and my records. That's all that was important to me I loaded up my '57 black Chevy sedan and backed it out of the garage. I came out of the bedroom with my hands full of clothes hangers. Lizzie was not surprised in the least to see me. "You fuck!" she blurted out, "I knew it."

I shot back, "You created everything, it was you who did this. You created everything you feared and supposedly dreaded the most. You made the situation."

She sat down at the kitchen table. I told her I would do her a favor and drop

Destiny back at the hospital. As I walked past her I heard, "Go, who the fuck would want you, anyway!" She started singing, "Hit the road Jack and don't you come back no more, no more, no

I simply shook my head and kept walking. She even got Lorrie to chime in with her, though I knew Lorrie would do whatever it took to stay on her mother's good side. Lizzie ended with "you're going to pay, pay, pay!"

Destiny and I were off now for the long ride back. Basically, our conversation was filled with small talk about the whole horrid situation. I begged her to please get her act together and straighten out. "You know your mother will not blink or hesitate to put you away again. You don't want to be spending your life in these places." Destiny agreed and reached to put the radio on, as we cruised up through Florida.

We heard the distinctive riffs of an organ. A song began and the chants of anguish started. Destiny and I looked at each other in dismay.

Too many teardrops for one heart to be crying

Too many teardrops, for one heart, to carry on. Your way on top now, since you left me you're always laughin, way down at me

But watch out now, I'm gunna get there

We'll be together, for just a little while

And then I'm gunna put you, way down here And you'll start cryin, 96 tears Cry, cry…

And when the sun comes up, I'll be on top You'll be right down there, lookin up And on my way, you come up here That I don't see you, wavin now I'm way down here, wonderin how I'm gunna get you…

But I know now.

I'll just CRY, cry, I'll just cry

Too many tear drops for one heart to be crying too many teardrops for one heart to carry on Your gunna cry, 96 tears

You gunna cry, 96 tears

Your gunna cry. Cry, cry, cry…

The lament continued, over and over. The song ended and would play again and again.

Destiny and I looked at each other. It was like it was directed at us. We felt like we drove into the Twilight Zone. For two hours to the door of the hospital we listened to the song. We hugged, kissed, held each other and said goodbye, with both of us wishing each other good luck. I drove off still listening to 96 Tears, well into the state of Georgia. Ironically this was the farewell song of a radio station going off the air and my farewell to the life I had been leading. Yet, like the songs unending cries it would become the theme of my life, repeating, repeating, and repeating. Always starting over with hopes "when the sun comes up, I'll be on top"

STARTING OVER

I headed north on 1-95, took a three-hour nap somewhere in the Carolinas and kept driving. I arrived at my sister's home about noon the next day. I was wiped out. I ran to the door of my sister's house, and she opened it in stunned disbelief to see me standing there

My sister MaryAnn and her family did all they could for me. I needed a plan to get started again of which I had none. I started to hang my hat wherever I could. Any friend who'd put me up. It was sometimes not the best of situations. Maybe I'd sleep in a basement or cellar, next to a boiler. I did whatever I had to do. My folks finally told me I was being foolish because I didn't want to trouble anyone. They told me to take the basement apartment in their home. It was where I grew up and would be a comfortable place to start again and heal emotionally.

That was the plan. My insurance ran out on my Chevy and I didn't want to make it a daily driver in the city. I walked to everything and took public transportation. I wasn't working, but the bills kept piling up. Lizzie forwarded everything to me—mortgage, utilities, credit cards, and especially hospital bills. The figures were astronomical! I had nothing but piles of paper and bills on my small kitchen table. I was depressed, stressed and tired. I didn't know how I'd ever get out of the mess I was in. My dad kept telling me to just do what I could, send something to Lizzie, just so they'd see I was making an effort.

In the meantime I was getting badgered with nuisance phone calls from Florida. My daughters would say obscene things. Lizzie was twisting their minds already Destiny started to taunt me with nasty phone calls, sometimes not hanging up the line for me to be able to make calls out. They'd call my mother to complain about me and all the family.

My mother must have been on the phone for an hour trying to put some sense into Lizzie's head when mom asked, "You are accusing my son of being an animal, but what did YOU do, Lizzie, to make Bobby this way?" I could almost hear Lizzie yelling through the phone "Fuck You!"

My mother responded "Fuck you, too!" I couldn't believe Lizzie yelled an obscenity at my mom and that my mother responded the same. Mom was visibly shaken when she got off the phone. I told her she should have hung up on Lizzie at the beginning of the conversation.

Things became so tense and frustrating that I actually ripped the phone out that I had down the basement and threw it out the cellar steps smashing it into pieces. Of course, to Lizzie and the kids everything was always my fault. I was frustrated and tired of defending myself. The best thing for me to do was cut ties for a while. I decided to just send letters back and forth to Eva. She was the youngest and was still innocent to a lot of what was going on. I could have communication with her without getting upset by the games and manipulation the girls were playing with me at their mother's manipulation.

I had to make arrangements to go back to Florida to pick up some of my belongings that Lizzie didn't want. A few pieces of family heirlooms, assorted bric-a-brac and furniture from my grandparents needed to be retrieved. Dad and I made the trip down. We rented a small truck. We were quick, in and out, with no words said to Lizzie. We strictly took care of business and were back North in a couple of days. It would be the start of a number of trips back and forth to Florida. It was time to find a lawyer. A lawyer I had consulted with in Brooklyn recommended that I wait for Lizzie to make a move for divorce papers first and that I seek counsel in Florida.

I was surprised when I was handed papers by a US marshal in the middle of Utica Avenue in East New York! Now I was forced to find counsel which was to be no easy feat. Most lawyers in Florida did not want to take on a client from out-of-state. Finally I found a lady lawyer who was head of the bar in Orlando. I had many a word with her as she seemed to be more on my wife's side than mine. I was just a voice on the phone to her and she never believed anything I told her till I saw her in person. Florida courts would go on to crucify me for the next four years!

Now my folks announced to me that they were going to sell the house we grew up in on E. 19th St. they were looking at retirement communities in New Jersey. I didn't know what I was going to do now. I had to continue to look for work. I would get up every day and walk through every neighborhood in and out of different repair shops looking for a hint of someone needing a transmission rebuilder. I walked from Gravesend to East New York, almost to Empire Boulevard.

Finally I landed a job in the transmission shop I had worked at once before but under new ownership. It was exciting to put some money back in my pocket. I had an extraordinary amount of bills and was in debt up to my eyeballs.

Things were starting to look up a little. I met a Spanish woman, Margarita, at a singles dance that my friend Carl dragged me to. We hit it off, and she insisted I move in with her and her two boys when my folks made the move to New Jersey. That provided some relief, overcoming my housing dilemma.

In the meantime I still walked and took public transportation everywhere. When I dated Margarita I walked and took two buses to pick her up. Sometimes she would foot for car service to wherever we were going. Margarita became very good for me. She calmed me and brought me back to the person I was before Lizzie had turned me into an animal.

I had also made friends with a guy named John at work. He liked me, and we lived in the same neighborhood so he started picking me up in the mornings on his way into the job saving me the long bus ride to East New York. John became very friendly with me and even wanted to set me up with his sister. I was wary about getting too close. For some reason I felt John was intimidated by me at work. We were both rebuilders at the shop. Maybe he realized I knew more than him and was afraid for his job for some reason.

One day the boss approached me and asked if I wanted a car that was left by a customer. It had been sitting for a couple of years and even had a transmission in it that I had done. I just had to reimburse him for the transmission and the car was mine. Wow! This gave me a new feeling of independence and freedom. My life was starting to get a little easier. But, I was still in tremendous debt. To try and alleviate my financial stress I went to visit some unsavory people I knew. Of course no problem, I could get the nut off my back and pay back later.

I finally moved in with Margarita. My folks were getting settled in their new home in New Jersey. Things seemed to be moving along, so I thought. I started making numerous trips to Florida. During court proceedings for divorce, they acted like I was on trial for murder. It was incredibly biased, I felt like they didn't believe a word I was telling them. My lawyer approached me and told me the court was in an uproar as to who to believe. It was a he said she said situation. She told me that they were intent on taking the girls and putting them in foster homes, since the family was so dysfunctional. I had to make a decision whether to succumb to all the accusations in order to keep the girls together under one roof. I had to save them from getting separated and put into foster homes.

That's exactly what I did to save my girls. I sat back, let them spew their lies, destroying me as a man, husband and father. Yes, yes! I was to blame for it all! Everything was my fault! I would agree to anything in order to spare my daughters.

I saved the children from a fate they never realized. But as for me, I lost everything. There was no 50% of anything. I was to pay all bills, child support, credit card debt or otherwise. They forced me to turn over two pieces of Florida property I owned and all stocks and bonds. Beside my own lawyer's fee, I was instructed to pay

$26,000 to her lawyer for his services. Even with all this Lizzie was still chasing me to take my veterans pension away.

I went through four years in court with Lizzie. The judge ordered the sale of the house in order to help pay off medical bills, because Lizzie was confused as to whether she should remain in the home with the kids or not, Imagine, confused? What an idiot! The judge told her to return my jewelry to me which she did on the last day of court proceedings. When all were dismissed, she approached me with a small box, handed it to me and quickly took off before I could even view the contents. She handed it to me,

"Here!" and ran out the door. Of course, when I opened it a number of things were missing.

What a piece of shit she was! Nothing was ever enough for her. She needed to steal some more. In the end Lizzie got all our personal belongings, furniture, and a lifetime of collectibles and antiques. $5000 came off the top of the sale of the house for her to move. The remaining proceeds, after all bills were paid by me, she received $30,000. I had tried my best to keep a line of communication open with my daughters. Many times letters or cards I sent would be returned in the mail unopened. Even Eva told me she always tried to sneak out of the house and get the mail before her mom did. Phone calls from the girls were a very rare and almost an impossible thing. This was Lizzie's way of punishing me, to keep me from my kids. She would constantly hang up on me when I called and asked to speak to the girls. If I had gotten one of them on the line already she would yank the phone out of their hands and hang up on me.

I had the opportunity to purchase a later model vehicle at a great price because it needed a transmission. When my shop got a little slow, my boss told me to bring it in and do the job. Of course as my luck would have it, while in the middle of rebuilding my transmission, we got pressed with other work. Now we needed my car off the lift in a hurry. So I took a part from one job I had on the bench and used it in mine to complete it faster and get it out of the shop. I would replace the part as I would continue working.

Well, this seemed like just the right opportunity now for my so-called friend John to go and tell the boss I was stealing from him. Of course I was called into the office, and I couldn't believe what I was accused of. I explained what I had done and that satisfied the situation. When I went to return to my bench I told John to stay away from me. He charged out of the booth he was working in and sucker punched me in the mouth. I attempted to retaliate but I had the entire rest of the crew pile up on me. Some friend, shake your one hand, stab you with the other.

Once again I was called to the office. The boss told me he had to let me go. I was getting the blame for the disturbance. I kept tabs on my friend John. It wasn't long before he had quit the job anyway, maybe a week or two later. He had been waiting on a manager job in a Ford dealership. Once I found out where he was, I made a phone call. There was more than one way to skin a cat. The following week John was let go. I understand he left for California after that.

Meantime, Destiny had left her mother. Run away, if you will. I told her she could not come to me because I'm sure her mother would make problems. Probably claim I kidnapped her. My sister MaryAnn was pregnant but offered to take Destiny in. I told Destiny to stay there till she was 18 and then -I'd make arrangements to have her come live with me. As I predicted, police showed up at my sister's door. MaryAnn told me the cops said they had better things to do than worry about a 16-year-old that was safe with family. With that they reported back to Florida.

I didn't find work right away, and to top it off went on a family picnic with Margarita. I started playing soccer, running around with 20-year-olds. When you're in your 40s and haven't played ball in years it's not the smartest thing to do, as I was soon to discover.

All at once I went down on one knee as I was wracked with pain. As I went to step off the ground, I thought I had been shot in the back of my right calf. It felt like a searing hot knife. I couldn't stand. The boys rushed me to a hospital emergency room. I had snapped my Achilles tendon. They put me in a soft cast and gave me directions. It had to heal on its own.

We went back to the picnic. Everyone tried to make me comfortable. I'd laid back on a recliner. Somebody brought me a beer and had placed it on a box next to me. I sat back, reached for the beer and started to drink. Yeow! There was a Yellow Jack on top of the can. Now I had gotten stung on the inside of my lower lip. When it rains it pours. You can't make this stuff up.

That was my luck. To say I felt miserable was an understatement.

Now I was forced to stay out of work. Things started to get really tight for us. Margarita worked privately as a cleaning woman. She had enough clientele to keep her busy all week. It just wasn't enough money to cover all living expenses. Finally the cupboard was bare. We needed to eat, so I started selling off my record collection. I let go of almost all my 78 RPM records selling early, vintage rock 'n roll and doo-wop treasures! But, we needed to eat and that was more important. As I started to heal I would go out and help Margarita take on some bigger specialty cleanup jobs. One place was a frat house that we refurbished.

Somehow we managed to get by. I was starting to get pressured by some of the characters I was indebted to. I kept them at bay and promised that I was good for the money. They knew me and had no problem. I explained the situation I was in. They understood. But there were people, friends or not, that you heeded lightly with because what was said and what could be done was another story.

Out of curiosity I walked into Rhythm Records on Avenue S. It was a record collectors' paradise with strictly rare rock 'n roll, rhythm and blues and doo-wop records from the late 40s to the mid-1960s. I had no money. But, just to go in and browse was a thrill for me. I had never been there before, though I knew of the store for years. I was always working with little time to window shop. I looked through rows of fantastic sounds. It was so exciting for me.

I always added to my wish list.

As I exited the store I noticed a small paper sign on the window. Someone was looking to form an acapella vocal group. I was interested so I walked back into the store and decided to ask the fellow behind the counter if he knew about it. His name was Charlie. He was a nice guy and told me he sang also. He asked for my number and told me he'd let me know when he got information about the group. I promised to come back and play a tape of a couple of songs I had recorded for ECI Studios in Long Island. I recorded these when I had first separated from Lizzie in an attempt to keep going and keep my mind off of my problems. I had always wanted to record songs with me doing lead, because in the past I had done mostly backup vocals.

I went back to the record shop the following weekend. Charlie was very

Impressed after hearing the tape and promised to call. "Nice Bobby, real nice!" I didn't hear from him for a while and figured it to be a dead-end like most times I tried to find singers, auditioned for, or put a group together myself.

About two months later I got a call from Charlie. He was putting together a jam session of different singers he knew and wanted to know if I was interested. I jumped at the chance to sing backup with guys that love doo-wop; it was a thrill! It was the early 90s, and the old sound wasn't really main stream anymore. When I got to Charlie's house I couldn't believe all the guys that showed up. I never realized how many people were still interested in the music.

It turned out to be a fantastic session. Charlie called me later to see what I thought. He wanted to have a group put together in the worst way. He wanted the right combination of people, and the blend had to be there. The blend we referred to was a sound produced by a certain combination of voices in vocal harmony. We continued getting together time after time trying different sessions with different people. We never seemed to achieve what we were looking for.

Finally I got another job at a Lee Miles shop on Coney Island Avenue. "On the Hill," we would say. It was a high spot in street elevation. There are not too many of those in Brooklyn. The place was right across the street from the old Kent movie theater. It brought back memories of 1961 when I saw "Birdman of Alcatraz" there with Burt Lancaster.

Even though I started working again, it wasn't enough. I was getting pressed by everyone I was in debt to. All the borrowing was catching up to me. I couldn't pay off fast enough. I was approached by two guys I didn't know one day and told that I should see my main lender. I did and he expressed faith in me, but he also remarked as I was leaving, "By the way, Bobby your girlfriend has nice legs."

With that I knew it was time to straighten my life out. My sister MaryAnn was also about to give birth and was pressing me to please take Destiny. She was of age and her strange behavior and habits were starting to weigh on my sister.

There was no room for Destiny with me at Margarita's place. It was a small apartment with the second bedroom shared by her two sons. I had to break the news to Margarita that I had to leave. I was worried about her and the two boys well-being after the remark I was told. Of course she was heartbroken but worst of all she didn't believe me. She thought I was making the whole thing up. It was very upsetting.

I woke up one day and sat on the edge of the bed thinking to myself. I have to get out of here. I felt it would be less traumatic to Margarita if I left when she wasn't there. So that's what I did. There wasn't much for me to take, just my clothes and records. My old Chippendale table I had salvaged from my marriage I left behind with Margarita. I was basically starting with nothing again. I only saw Margarita for a few times more after I left. She was very hurt. But it was the best way I knew to keep her safe.

I found a two-bedroom, top floor, rear apartment at the end of West Street off of Avenue U in Gravesend. It would be perfect for me, a good place to live, away from the rest of the world, until I straightened my life out. I went in there with absolutely nothing. It's amazing all the things you take for granted until you don't have them. A simple bar of soap, sponge, utensils, you name it, I didn't have it. I slept on the bare wood floor in the living room at night. Even though it was April I couldn't sleep and had the chills all night because I had no blanket or pillow. All my money was going to those I owed. But, I finally started to make some headway on some of the basics.

I finally bought a bed with sheets and blankets, pillows, the works. I only slept in it a couple of nights. I had Destiny come to live with me and I gave my daughter the bed. I went back to the living room floor. Little by little with the help of people giving me things I began to live normally. I took other people's clothes, pots and pans, anything they were willing to give, I took.

After about four months in the apartment, the doorbell rang. I peered through the front door window but was not able to see who was standing there. The box the person is holding is covering their upper torso. I opened the door to find my brother Stevie's voice asking, "How long are you going to go on without a TV?!" I was flabbergasted and excited. My brother had bought us a TV. I was so grateful!

"Normal" was the definitive word. That's all I was ever looking for but it wasn't to be. Destiny and her behavior were stranger than ever. First thing I noticed within the first two weeks she was there with me was a faint smell of vomit in the bathroom. I questioned her about it, of course, with denials from her. Then I was even starting to see remains of feces not cleaned off the back wall behind the toilet. I was no idiot. I knew what was going on. I started finding empty packages of Ex-Lax, 90 pills, gone... imagine?! ..I had nothing but stress and insanity again. Destiny would eat chicken, and I would find the bones back in the refrigerator. She'd eat an apple, and I would find the core placed back in the fruit bin.

I asked her why she was doing this stuff. She didn't know. She'd eat hot cocoa mix, the powder out of the can along with bags of sugar. I knew she was bulimic. I asked her, "For all the time you lived with your mother, she never realized you had a problem? I'm a man and I knew something was wrong right after you moved in. You know we're going to get you help!"

With all this going on I was working my butt off. As I started to get on my feet, I began going out on the weekends. I was getting involved with more and more women. I kept hearing my ex's voice in my head as I walked out the door, "Who the fuck would want you anyway?"

It was almost as if I had to prove something to myself, that I was desirable. But it got out of hand. The stress at home with Destiny seemed to be pushing me more and more into this pattern of behavior. I was becoming a real ladies man. I never had to approach a woman; for some reason they always approached me, I was so glad because I wasn't a pickup artist, but I guess I made the girls feel comfortable. The thing was I lost control of it all. I had so many girl friends; I was finding they had the same first names, so I started numbering them.

Destiny couldn't believe it either. One day a car pulled alongside me as I drove with Destiny in the passenger seat, three women looked right past Destiny trying to pick me up. Destiny remarked, "Oh my God dad, I can't believe it, the girls love you, it's crazy!"

What was crazy though, was my life with my daughter Destiny. I started attending all kinds of counseling groups with her. Anorexia, bulimia, and so many kinds of people, attended these meetings. I was in shock that people my age and even men had the problem. It was so sad. I wanted my daughter better in the worst way.

Amidst all of this Charlie called me and told me he met an interesting guy named Paul at his chiropractor's office. He sang with a group called "Jump Street." They were looking for a first tenor. If I was interested I could go down and audition. I picked Charlie up, and he took me to meet the group. It was terrific! I fit right in. The blend and the fit overall were good; they were nice guys.

"JUMP STREET"
*Left to Right: Carlos Rampolla, Paul Rothenburg, Tommy Horlic,
Charlie Piacentino, Bobby Monti*

In the meantime Charlie still wanted us to pursue a group of our own. I started doing gigs with Jump Street and felt a surge of exhilaration, I continued to pursue different combinations of singers for Charlie and me to have our own group.

I had Destiny in and out of all kinds of therapy groups. She was driving me mad. She was getting worse. She was supposed to be on different medications, which they kept changing all the time. She was living in the dark at home. I found a suit case under the bed with empty beer bottles and half eaten pizza pies in boxes. We started having mice. My liquor cabinet was emptied. I would find hashish and pot wrapped in tinfoil under her pillow. She was having friends over that I didn't approve of.

I found out later that they had stolen a number of my collectible records. It became total chaos in the house with Destiny lashing out at me, spewing all the crap her mother fed her. Things were so extreme that she would not leave the apartment at all.

She asked me, "Daddy, please get me a pack of cigarettes at the corner." After I rushed down the block to get the cigarettes, I realized I forgot my house keys. I banged on the door, rang the bell, and yelled for a half-hour before my daughter came to the door, hiding under a blanket like a bogeyman was about to get her. She was out of control, and I was forced to admit her to Maimonides Hospital at the urgency of one of her counseling psychiatrists. The deadly combinations of illegal drugs she was taking mixed with alcohol and prescriptions put her on the brink of a heart attack, so I had no choice. She had to stay six weeks in the hospital .That was the program.

Of course, I visited with her often, but she was a mess. It seemed to be that once she got past a certain downward point she would try hard to straighten out. She told me what she wanted was to get her life on track going in the right direction. I believed it did no harm to try to be as supportive as possible.

I called Charlie up and told him I had a combination of guys in mind that might possibly work out for a good group, so I set everything up. Charlie, Stevie, Patrick, me and a friend I made at the Town Café in Sheepshead Bay, Michael Sarzano, were the choice picks. Michael sang and recorded with his own group many years earlier, "Michael and The Continentals," and his brothers who were very well known as the "Bay Bops" recorded quite a few records back in the day.

As I drove for Charlie on the way to Michael's where we were getting together, Charlie asked me who I had coming. As I mentioned Mikey Sarzano to him, Charlie repeated "Mikey Sarzano! Whooa, Bobbeeeee stretching my name out with his gravelly voice. "Pull over, pull over. Mikey Sarzano?! Do you know who he is?"

I turned to him looking surprised, "Yeah, I know who he is. Is it a problem?" "Noooo, the guy is great. You know him, how do you know him? How'd you find him? Oh my God, I can't believe you Bobbeeeee!" Charlie continued, outlandishly.

Charlie was very animated about the evening, to say the least. The evening worked out well, and we all decided to meet each week and start rehearsing. Charlie and I also started singing with a couple of fellows we knew in Greenpoint. Another Mike, a friend of Charlie's, invited us. This was a group in progress also. John, formerly of "Egg Cream" was looking for a particular sound, too. Charlie and I were in and two other fellows, John and Victor.

I started singing with so many different groups I couldn't remember what arrangement to what song was with which group. As fate would have it John's group "Mystique" was not for me. I moved on and eventually so did Charlie. The two of us continued to put combinations of different singers together. The singers we put in place originally didn't come to pass. Michael Sarzano and the group we put together fell apart with a lot of discourse amongst singers.

I continued to perform with "Jump Street." We were appearing professionally in many different venues. Even there I never realized that problems loomed behind the scenes with the members before I got there. As I tried to bring the group to a new level, everything fell apart.

I took the group out to my friend's studio in Massapequa Long Island. Michael Capitan was an old friend who had recorded my original group "the Apostles". I thought I could take "Jump Street" to new heights in music. That night at the studio, the animosity between everyone surfaced and "Jump Street's" demise became inevitable.

Tommy and Paul of "Jump Street" still had a remaining major gig to fulfill at Tarrytown Music Hall. Tommy approached me and asked if I knew anyone else that would blend with us so we could continue on and fulfill the commitment. I mentioned Charlie to them, and we made arrangements to get together. We were experimental with different arrangements and songs.

Before the night was through we sat inside the car still singing. Tommy was trying to figure out what to do because Pauli and Charlie were both baritones. He and I were tenors. I did first and Tommy second. We started another tune when Charlie decided to jump to the top and do over tenor. It clicked.

"Oh my God!" Tommy snapped. "I think we've got something."

Charlie always had a fantastic and distinctive over tenor. This was coming closer to the sound we were looking for, but we needed a base. Charlie remembered Carlos, another singer we knew who was floating with groups. Yes, I agreed 100%. Carlos was a second tenor, but could do a great base. He had the range and knew all the moves. "Jump Street" was reborn that night.

So electrify! We did a number of studio rehearsals. We sounded great and we were all psyched. We opened the show at a packed house in Tarrytown, being introduced as the best a cappella group in the country. We lived up to our introduction. We opened for the "Solitaires," "Earl Lewis and the Channels," and "Johnny Maestro and the Brooklyn Bridge." What a feeling!

The house lights were dimmed; the Hall was silent. I handled the mic since I would begin the show's first song, "Wonderful Girl" by the "Five Satins." I dedicated it to all the wonderful girls in the audience. In the dead silence I began "Kiss... my... lips..." hearing my voice echoing all alone, and the first chord of harmony broke out! I had goose bumps on my arms. The audience loved it! To share the stage with groups we idolized was a thrill of a lifetime for us.

We continued as "Jump Street" only for a short time. Pauli was having personal problems and looking to move to Florida. He was the first to leave and then Tommy jumped ship. I think Tommy didn't want to sing without Pauli. They had been close friends over the years. So Charlie, Carlos and I continued to audition new singers. I was determined to put my own group together. I knew if I could have a great group with the right people and sound that we could go places. I had all the connections after being in the loop for so long.

Destiny would soon be getting out of the hospital, and my daughter Lorrie was going to come up for a visit. I asked Lorrie if her mother had ever taken her to the doctor as she had an issue that was important to her, a lady problem, if you will. She told me her mother had never taken her. I had sent some funds to my ex for this purpose and had just received the canceled check back five months later deposited into her personal account. I assured Lorrie that her needs would be taken care of when she arrived here in Brooklyn.

Destiny was released from the hospital. She seemed better for a little while and then started to slide back to the same nonsense. When Lorrie arrived, I took her to the doctors first thing. She spent a few weeks with us and saw for herself what was going on. I was in and out of outpatient clinics with Destiny. She had standard appointments every week. They waited to speak with her to see where she was emotionally, as well as monitor her medication.

It was 98 degrees and Destiny would wear a long, bulky woolen sweater, holding down the sleeves with the palms of her hands. It seemed peculiar to me, and I asked her if she was hot. I asked the doctor how he saw her progress and how he thought she was doing. He felt she was on the right path and that she was doing extremely well. I was very happy to hear that, but my instincts seemed to be telling me there was something wrong

I came home from work a few nights later to find all of my pain medication from the Veterans Hospital had disappeared. I was troubled. I questioned Destiny. Of course, she didn't know anything about it. Lorrie said to me, "Daddy, don't you know what's going on? She tried to kill herself the other night! Why do you think she's been wearing these long sleeved sweaters?" "What?" I said as I turned and looked at Destiny who sat on the edge of the bed. I grabbed her arms pulling up her sleeves. She was bandaged from her wrist to her elbows. Lorrie had bandaged her. As I pulled back the dressing, I saw that Destiny had cut herself deeply with razor blades on both arms and would be scarred for life.

I was beyond disturbed by all of this—her lying to me and deceiving the doctor.

This showed how much he knew! As a professional and aware of these issues you would have thought he would have questioned Destiny on her choice of fashion and looked into it more deeply.

I was so angry and upset with her. In my frustration I grabbed her, put her over my knee, and spanked her like a little child, yelling at her to get her act together as she screamed. I told her she was 20 years old now and an adult. She needed to know and understand there were consequences for her actions in life. When was she going to get it?

I asked her how she could lie to me about my medications after Lorrie told me she took them all. -.1 had assured Lorrie, Destiny didn't do such a thing; if she had taken them all, she wouldn't be with us right now. I believed she was looking for attention. I asked Destiny if this was the kind of attention she was after, the negative sort. I finally hugged her as she stood there crying. I felt guilty as hell for spanking her. I don't know what came over me in my moment of rage. I was just so frustrated with her.

Lorrie finally left to return to Florida, and my life with Destiny continued in a vicious spiral, constantly seeking professional help and starting at square one. It was starting to affect me. I was getting blood blisters in my mouth and profuse nose bleeds out of the blue. I'd be rehearsing, and in the middle of singing, I'd get a nose bleed. I was driving home from work one day, and as I stopped for a light, blood just seemed to gush from my face. I reached for clean shop towels I had on the seat next to me, drenching them. My nose was pouring so profusely, I had to pull over. I sat for a half hour swallowing my own blood. It seemed like I couldn't get it to stop. I knew I had to see a doctor. I made quite a number of visits until they cauterized all my blood vessels.

SUMMER KNIGHTS
Top Left to Right: Charlie Piacentino, Patrick DePrisco
Bottom Row Left to Right: Carlos Rampolla, Cal NG, Bobby Monti

ONE SUMMER KNIGHT

Even with all the constant stress, I never stopped moving forward in my life. I continued to put in many hours at work and did side jobs whenever I could. Finally, I found two more singers that would blend with Charlie, Carlos, and myself—Patrick, a second tenor, and Cal, a baritone.

We got together for a rehearsal at Cal's home. Wow! We had something.

It was time to get serious. We rehearsed weekly, twice a week. We were going places and fast. I started booking jobs—restaurants, lounges, clubs. Carlos also booked some work such as pool and beach clubs and store openings. Everyone loved us. We were booked for big shows, opening for all the great and legendary groups. I got the guys into the studio, and we recorded a demo tape of six songs. This attempt was, in part, the big door opener for us. We had a very distinct street sound. The amazing thing about the group was that all five members could do lead, and we would still maintain the same sound. We were "Summer Knights!"

Back at home Destiny continued to drive me crazy. I finally collapsed from all the stress. I don't know what came over me. While sitting on the bedroom floor talking to Destiny and watching TV, I keeled over, lying on the floor not being able to move. I didn't know what was wrong with me, and neither did Destiny. She called my friend Carl, who rushed over. He stood over me and asked me questions. I don't remember answering. I just stared at him blankly. Carl called an ambulance telling the EMT I was lethargic and not moving. As the EMT carried me out on a stretcher, he said, "You know, when people tell you to take it easy or you're going to end up in the hospital, well you did it, pal!"

I don't recall if Destiny came with me in the ambulance or followed with Carl to the Veterans Hospital. All I knew was that she was there in the emergency room with me till four in the morning. She apologized for everything. I knew it was breaking her heart to see me like this, and I also knew she just couldn't control herself. By 4 a.m. I was feeling much better. I guess I simply needed to relax and rest. I got up and walked out of the emergency room, went home, changed my clothes, and went to work. Some would say I was a little crazy, too, but I couldn't afford to lose a day's pay by not going in. That would just be more stressful a situation.

My new group "Summer Knights" continued to make music as more and more doors opened for us. My love life was getting more complicated. Financially I kept moving in the right direction, slowly getting back on my feet. The group is what kept me going as I spent more time with Destiny. There were endless visits to clinics, doctors, counseling, and all leading to one place. Back into the hospital she went, I tried to be supportive and help her in every way a father could, but it was up to her to get her head straight. I realized I couldn't go on living like this anymore. When it came time for Destiny to be released again, of course, hospital personnel told me she'd be fine and had rehabilitated well. I told her doctor that there was no place on the outside to care for her. I lied and told them that I wasn't living at home and had moved in with my girlfriend.

They told me that they were putting Destiny into a program and would find a home for her in an adult living facility that would care for all her medical needs, keeping her on track. The facility was set up like a home. She would have her own room and be free to come and go as she pleased with their knowledge. There were rules to follow, and it would be exactly what she needed, saving me from a nervous breakdown.

Time went on. Destiny was eager to leave the hospital. I insisted she wait for her social service representative to come through. Every time I asked, they told me they were waiting on a bed. There were no openings yet, and there was a wait list. This went on for as long as I could delay the inevitable. I knew once I took Deserie home that life would slowly slip back to the way it was. It always did. My hand was forced as I was told to take her home since we were still waiting for a bed, and it wasn't in her best interest to remain in that environment.

It wasn't long before my daughter and I were at each other's throats. All the same loony stuff went on daily--eaten food put back in the fridge and leftovers placed under the bed; living in the dark; her bulimia still out of control. Binge and purge! Binge and purge! Whatever she didn't vomit up came out the other end as she abused laxatives. I couldn't handle her bipolar ways anymore. She was diagnosed with this and her meds never seemed to do what they were supposed to. How could they?

All my liquor disappeared, and besides the drinking, she was doing other drugs. I didn't know what types of drugs, and I just didn't care anymore. Cleaning up her bathroom messes had me disgusted. She had turned my home into a mice-ridden pig sty. I'd finally had it! At my wit's end, I told Destiny if she didn't leave and find a place, then I would leave. As I told her this, .1 glanced down at the bed I had given her and what were once beautiful new bed sheets. Now they were filled with cigarette burn marks. I told her she was going to burn the house down and to stop smoking in bed. She told me, "I know," opening the top of her blouse showing me the burn mark on her chest that she did to herself by falling asleep while smoking. I just shook my head.

It seemed I was in a dysfunctional household again, and it was Destiny and me. The crap that her mother poisoned her with spewed from her mouth every time I walked in the door, as her words to me mimicked her mother's when we lived together. I gave her ample time to find an apartment. Somehow I knew her leaving was never going to happen. It was time for me to save myself once again. I was starting to get very sick and was stressed all the time.

At work my boss kept pushing me to produce more and more. The whole shop seemed to rely mostly on my expertise. From the moment I walked into work my name was called for everything. I couldn't handle much more. My boss Paul approached me and said, "What is it, you want more money?"

"No!" 1 responded. "You're not getting it. I'm only one person. No matter what you pay me, I can only do so much."

I picked up the church paper every week looking for apartments, finally finding a good one. A young woman had just bought a house in Gravesend and remodeled the whole place. It was a top floor apartment. Beautiful! it had new Italian tiles throughout, a new bathroom and kitchen and was perfect for me. I would even be in control of my own heat.

I informed Destiny that I was moving out. She wasn't sure what she was going to do. I told her as I always did, "God helps those who help themselves, and so do dads!" Whether she understood it or not,

I didn't know. I had the rent paid, and she had a month's security, which would give her an extra month's time to figure it out.

I turned over about $1,000 in leftover funds from her social security disability payments that I had gotten for her. It had helped me pay for a lot of her doctor bills and medication, since I was always taking it out of my own pocket. It was time to grow up; she was old enough.

I didn't have much to take with me. I tried to leave some things so Destiny could take care of herself. I left her the bed, telling her to use it until she was ready to move. Then I would reclaim it. I had a futon that my cousin had sold to me, an entertainment center, and of course, what was left of my record collection. I left her enough pots, pans, and dishes, along with all the groceries and dry goods. It was easier for me that way, also. I'd move with nothing and start over again.

After all this, I developed a sleeping disorder. I never slept anymore through the night. As much as I was excited about my new apartment, I felt like I was walking around zombie-like.

I couldn't think straight. I was exhausted between my job and personal life.

The phone rang. It was my landlord from the apartment I had shared with Destiny. He asked me if I wouldn't mind coming by; he needed to speak to me. When I met with him, he was upset but understanding that he rented me the apartment and that I had walked away leaving Destiny behind.

He informed me that Destiny had taken in a girlfriend as a roommate. who assumed the apartment belonged to her. The friend began taking control, calling authorities on the landlord for whatever ills existed in the apartment, most of which were created by my daughter.

I reassured the landlord that I would take care of everything. He wanted Destiny and her girlfriend out. I paid him for another month's rent, and then I went up the stairs to speak to both of them. As I entered, I was aghast at how disheveled and filthy the place was. As I looked around, I noticed my bed was gone.

"Where's my bed?" I demanded to know.

"I sold it." Destiny said.

"You sold it!! The bed wasn't yours to sell. Destiny! That was my bed that I was nice enough to let you sleep on." I couldn't believe what she had done.

Destiny's girlfriend was older than she was. But now I needed to reprimand both of them, like two children. I told Destiny's friend she was just a guest there, and that it wasn't her place to instigate or lodge complaints to authorities about an apartment that wasn't hers. It was Destiny's responsibility to take care of. I had left HER with the apartment.

I told Destiny that if she had any beef, she should learn to speak up and talk to the landlord on her own. I then let them know I paid for another month's rent, but they had to get out. I wasn't bailing them out anymore. They were thankful and apologetic, telling me they'd be out in time. I walked out in disbelief that my daughter had sold my bed!

My life always seemed to be spiraling out of control. I was so tired due to not sleeping at night. I was still being pressured at work. Finally Bruce, the service manager, had some comments to me which were sarcastic, though he meant them in a joking way.

I had had enough. I felt like I was coming apart at the seams. I was feeling drained and sick all the time. I responded to him very negatively.

"You know what, Bruce? Get yourself another asshole!" That was it for me. I quit.

Bruce called me even though I quit. He always liked me, and seemed to know what I was going through. He kept in touch, basically with the intention of starting his own business and wanting me to work for him.

My nights became even longer with no sleep. Nights turned into days, days into nights. I sought help and was trying natural things to help me relax. I would wander the apartment in the evenings watching old movies to pass the time. I never thought I'd be up at three a.m. watching "March of the Wooden Soldiers."

One night at 1:15 a.m. my girlfriend Debbie called to tell me that Destiny was out of control. She had been calling Debbie the last few nights but Debbie didn't want to alarm me. Debbie figured she could handle Destiny. But tonight was different. Destiny called Debbie very late, waking and disturbing her household, looking for me, spewing venom and cursing me.

Debbie said, "Bobby, you'd better call her and see what is bothering her. She can't keep calling here like this!"

I apologized to Debbie and told her I'd take care of it.

I called Destiny. She was like a raving lunatic, not making any sense. She kept yelling at me, at the top of her lungs, at 1:30 in the morning! She accused me of "dissing" her. I dissed her? I had no Idea what she was talking about. I couldn't get a straight answer out of her. nor could I calm her down.

I shouted back, "Don't make me come over there. What is your problem?"

She accused me of all kinds of things that I had no clue what she was referring to.

"Destiny, please stop it," I implored.

"Fuck you, Dad, fuck you!"

That was it. I slammed the phone down and charged out of the house. I was tired and so enraged! I still had the key to the foyer door for the apartment I left Destiny in. Running two steps at a time up the stairs, I banged on the apartment door. I yelled and screamed for Destiny to open it. She had it locked and chained from the inside.

I kept yelling for her to open the door. I told her that if she didn't open the door, I was going to break it down. I continued to bang and yell for her to open the door, becoming even more enraged. I broke through the door, slicing my forearm open as it blasted through. Destiny had wedged herself behind the door. The moldings ripped from the door jam and the chain broke from the strength of my anger.

As I plowed through the door, it smacked Destiny in the face, bloodying her nose. .1 ran in and smacked her in the face for cursing at me. I yelled at her for tormenting my girlfriend's family every night. There was blood everywhere from my arm and Destiny's nose bleed. Glasses full of soda broke as Deserie flung them wildly at me, hitting the walls. Glass was shattering across the hallway and kitchen. I was on the brink of insanity. I screamed, yelled. and reprimanded her at two in the morning.

She picked up the phone and called the cops.

"Go ahead, call the cops, and just get the hell out of my life! Straighten yourself out and leave people alone!" I was exhausted as I looked around the place. What started out as a cute apartment was now totally destroyed. Destiny sat at the top of the stairs as I stepped over her to leave. She waited for the police to arrive.

I continued to get phone calls from Bruce, but now it was in regard to the police inquiries. He told me they were looking for me, and they were repeatedly coming to the shop asking questions. Also, he had heard from my girlfriend who was also being visited by police. He told me it was very embarrassing for her having police visiting her home. Her neighbors were talking.

I got in touch with Debbie. She felt sorry for me and was upset about the whole situation. She asked me if I could talk to the police and let them know what happened so they would stop harassing her. As always, once again, I promised to take care of it.

1 was concerned that they had issued a warrant for my arrest. I spoke to Bruce once more. He told me that the police were visiting him once again. They told him there was no warrant for my arrest. They only wanted to speak with me. I didn't believe any of it, but I was feeling terrible that everyone was being interrogated. I decided to call the precinct and ask for the detective who left his name with Bruce. I called from an outside line, not trusting anyone.

I spoke to the detective, and he assured me I wouldn't be arrested. He simply wanted to hear my side of the story. So I set up a time to see him. I was extremely leery and apprehensive about the whole thing.

The next day I walked into the precinct on Coney Island Avenue. I announced who I was to the desk sergeant and asked for the detective. He nodded his head and two officers approached me from behind, grabbing my arms and cuffing my wrist behind my back "I thought I wasn't going to be arrested!"

The officers did not respond as they marched me into a cell. "Those lying sacks of shit!" I thought to myself. I sat in the cell for hours with a couple of fools who were in trouble. Finally, the detective I was to see showed up.

"Mr. Monti- come with me," he led me out of the cell.

I told him, "I thought I wasn't going to be arrested."

"Well, we can't take any chances, you understand," he shrugged.

"Yeah. I understand." I answered, sarcastically.

The two of us sat off in a small room as he began to question me. I didn't lie or hold back anything as I recounted my story. When I finished, the detective looked up at me and said, "I understand completely. I'm a father also. If I was in the situation, I'd have done the same thing! "Then he informed me that I would have to go before the judge and see what he makes of things.

The police escorted me back to the cell. It was early evening now. An officer came and removed me and two others from the cell. They handcuffed us and shackled us together at the ankles with chains. They led us out onto the street where a paddy wagon awaited. I walked with my head down; I was mortified that someone in the neighborhood would see me. We stepped up into the paddy wagon, chaining us to the rest of the crew that was inside. With nowhere to sit. I stood to the back and tried to hold on and keep from losing my balance as the wagon sped off down the road.

The next stop was central booking downtown Brooklyn. What a freaking nightmare! We were marched down to cells in single file, put into 10' x 12' rooms with open latrines, the cells filled to the brim with every low life in town. It was filthy and disgusting, with no room for another person to stand. They squeezed us in anyway. I stood there wedged between other bodies, watching as fights broke out and listening to guys who thought they were tough brag about how many times they'd been in the slammer. What idiots! This was nothing to brag about.

It was one of the most humiliating experiences of my entire life. At about three in the morning, officers came around offering apples, milk and bologna sandwiches. I took nothing even though I hadn't eaten in hours. I stood in place, sleepless all night as a million thoughts passed through my head. I came to the realization that everyone had lied to me, and that's exactly what I should do if necessary when I went before the judge that next day.

I was appointed a public defender who met with me just prior to appearing before the judge. He tried to advise me and told me it would be best if I just pled guilty to the charges of assault and battery and breaking and entering. Imagine! Breaking and entering into my own apartment, one that I paid the rent for!

I was called to appear. I stood there silently looking toward the bench. "Mr. Monti." the Judge began.

"Yes, your honor?"

"I'm reading your files. I see you're a 45 year old man with a clean record. Do you want to tell me what happened? You are being accused of assault!"

"Your honor, I have no idea. My daughter is bi-polar and bulimic and being treated. She takes medications for her problems, but is also doing drugs. Maybe her boyfriend hit her and she thought it was me."

"You have no idea what went on?" the judge probed.

"No, your honor, not at all."

"I'm going to release you on your own recognizance. You're to appear before me along with your daughter next month. The court officer will give you the date. That's all." The judge waved his arm, dismissing me.

"Thank you, your honor." I walked away humbly, cursing him and everyone who had lied to me.

I returned home relieved to be free, vowing to myself that I would somehow change my life. For the next 12 months, I would visit the courts on my appointed day. My public defender advised me to plead guilty. He said they were looking to put me away for seven years; they were looking to throw the book at me. I told the defender I was only guilty of being a father. Let my accuser show up, look me in the eye, and point the finger at me. I knew it would never happen. I knew my daughter well.

She never showed up for one appearance through the entire process. After a year of my reporting, they dismissed the case, and I walked away with a clear record.

SUMMER KNIGHTS

Now with extra time on my hands the year would provide opportunities for me to move my group, "Summer Knights," forward. Not wanting to forget about having to earn a living, I racked my brain thinking of something else I could do other than transmission work. I went into what I thought was a good opportunity developing a gourmet coffee route.

Looking back. I realized I wasn't thinking clearly at the time. My sleepless nights had caught up to me. and the stress of everything I had been through wore me down. I also had a habit of panicking whenever I was out of work. This left me with poor judgment. I invested thousands of hard earned dollars into selling coffee. In disbelief. I watched as a huge tractor trailer pulled up to my apartment to deliver endless cases of coffee and coffee displays. I had to accept the order and didn't know where I was putting it all. I was worried my new landlord would see this stuff coming into my apartment.

I have to laugh. I filled my entire apartment to the ceiling in every room. Leaving just enough space in between boxes to make a path through the apartment by walking sideways. I was to sell the coffee locally, but it wasn't moving. I had to pull all the stands and displays I'd set up in stores, discarding them in any dumpsters I could find. I couldn't seem to sell the route, either. I ended up with a lifetime supply of coffee for my personal use. I sold it off, eventually, to friends and family, but not without a great personal loss of my investment.

Once again, I was to start over.

My extra time at home afforded me the chance to do a lot of leg work for Summer Knights. I was making connections like mad. We had taken off like a rocket! Steady gigs were happening every weekend. From high-end Penthouses in Manhattan, to New York City clubs and South Street Seaport, we were booking in all five boroughs. We opened many big shows for legendary Doo Wop groups.

A number of clubs wanted to book us steady every weekend. I had to refuse; we had so much work. I didn't want to get locked into being a house group. We were invited on Don K. Reed's Doo Wop

Shop, CBS FM. N. Y. on Sunday night. It was very exciting. Also. we did Mickey B's Juke Box Review radio show on WGBB Long Island, NY.

I spent an entire year working on getting us a spot on ABC Television with Bill Evans in the morning. We were riding high, and I had many visions for the group, including coming out with original material. Beside the excitement, we were having fun and the time of our lives! Everything I ever fantasized about singing when I was a kid was coming true. It was a thrill of a lifetime to work with all of the great recording artists I idolized as a kid. We opened for many of the greats including Johnny Maestro & The Brooklyn Bridge, Passions, Capris, Drifters, Earl Lewis & The Channels, Duprees, Classics, Larry Chance & The Earls, Mystics, Five Discs, Reparata & The Del Rolls, Vito & The Salutations, The Tokens and The Shangdlas!

We were playing a local Italian restaurant on Kings Highway, and some friends of Charlie's came to see us. I was introduced to a young lady named Dora who told me she was a singer also. She was with a dance band and performed at weddings. She asked me if I would like to come see her group audition for couples getting married at a large catering hall, on Avenue U, on the west side. She seemed to be a nice person so I went. I took a seat at a table with the rest of the couples. Dora came over to say hello and seemed to go out of her way for me. She kept referring to me as honey and made me a cocktail as her group was about to perform. She was the lead singer and very good. My first impression was that she reminded me of Teresa Brewer. She had that kind of sound.

"SUMMER KNIGHTS"
Left to Right: Patrick DePrisco, Cal NG, Bobby Monti, Carlos Rampolla, Charlie Piacentino

She was happy and surprised that I came to see her. She thanked me and gave me her number. I started dating her along with a number of other girlfriends I had.

Summer Knights continued to perform. We continued to open shows. We did some weddings and benefits for people who had encountered hardships. We'd raise cash and sing off the cuff. One of the strangest gigs for me was a time we were requested to sing at a wake, right next to the casket. It was the eeriest thing I ever did. It was so strange to sing over a dead person. The family of the deceased loved it!

Of course. Singing with four other people had its moments. It was like being married and much compromise was needed. Cal had lost his home and job. He ended up in the projects in Coney Island. If he needed something for his place, I gave whatever I could. We'd perform at a job, and he needed a belt for his pants, I'd bring him one and give it to him. Cal also started becoming a little insecure as we followed different groups in a playbill. He'd worry that we couldn't cut it, but we always did and usually stole the show

As a matter of fact other groups would usually admire us and compliment us about how great they thought we were. It was a nice feeling to hear that. Patrick, our second tenor, also in a dance band and Carlos was starting to get upset that Patrick was never willing to concede a job to us when his band was booked on the same evening. That forced us to get fill ins. Charlie was always Charlie, down on his luck, never had much money and always struggling to get by. I always helped him also. He had no car so I picked him up for rehearsals and gigs and brought him home. Everyone owned his own microphone but him. So I bought him one.

Charlie always managed to give us a laugh though. If we were doing a gig and the group was dressed in black trousers, Charlie would walk out of the house with brown pants on. I'd make him go back in the house, iron his pants and change. If we showed up in Manhattan with everyone carrying their outfits in dry cleaning plastic, pressed and ready, Charlie showed up with his clothes rolled up inside a paper bag.

Dora and I had hit it off. We started to get romantically involved and would go to each other's gigs. That became hectic as it was very time consuming. Cal started to ask Dora to do a few leads with us. It was a nice novelty and people enjoyed it, but some of the guys resented it. We were our own entity. I really don't know why Cal kept asking Dora to sing; I could see it wasn't serving in our best interest. This came to a head when Cal asked Dora to appear on a big card with us. We featured her on our arrangement of "Till" by the Angels. Cal suggested we all take money out of our pay in order to give Dora something. She was singing with us for the fun of it and didn't want any pay. This ignited a lot of tension in the group. I asked Dora to turn down any further requests by Cal.

I decided to ask Dora to marry me. She had never been married and was approaching her forties. She wanted a family and seemed to come from a good background. I was family oriented and enjoyed coming home to a wife and kids. With Lizzie cutting me off from my children I saw it as a fresh start. I asked Dora to marry me in church at mass one Sunday. I thought it might help if I did it before God.

We went through all the usual preparations for marriage. The only thing I didn't want to do was give up the beautiful apartment I had on Lake Street. Everything was brand new and modern. Dora insisted I move in with her as her grandmother just gave her money for new carpeting that she had already put down. This made her resistant to leave her own apartment.

No sooner had life started settling down, Dora decided to quit her day job.

Suddenly she couldn't take talking to people after being a receptionist for years. Here we go again! I'm always carrying the load alone. Then she had this brainstorm that she wanted to be a cosmetologist and do women's makeup. She wanted to work for herself. This takes schooling and who had to pay for it all? Yours truly! Plus, now I had to come up with money for her parent's 50th wedding anniversary. As for myself, well I've gone back to transmission rebuilding, working for a friend of Dora's who owned a shop in Bensonhurst.

Singing with our groups continued on a major scale. I got a call one day from the producer of Starlight records offering a CD deal to Summer Knights. I actually dropped the phone along with my jaw as I got so incredibly excited! I listened with my mouth open as he explained how he wanted to feature us on our own CD. This was an honor, because the company usually put out compilations of groups on a disk.

The producer was very enthusiastic and impressed with us. We went to meet with him, but it looked like the project was going to the back burner. Most of our group felt that they couldn't come up with the couple of hundred bucks each that we would need to chip in and get the ball rolling. The producer was willing to bear the brunt of the expense. We also had gotten an offer to work Atlantic City casinos, but we had to pay for our own room and board. I tried to convince the guys into doing it, just to get our foot in the door.

At about the same time we performed on a show In Staten island where we featured Dora. I was approached by a record producer from All Rs Records. He liked our stage presence and harmonies. He wanted to hear Dora with her dance band. What he offered was to write songs för Dora on lead. backed by Summer Knights vocally and Dora³s dance band as the musicians.

Now, he felt he had a self-contained troop. He wanted to know that if we had a hit and anything broke would we all be willing to tour together. I approached Summer Knights with this and they were willing to go. Next we had set up a meeting with Dora's group, Backstage Pass, at a rehearsal studio one night. During a break I introduced Fred the producer from All Rs Records, and he explained everything in detail.

His speech was met with much suspicion and questions from Backstage Pass. The outcome was a blatant no from all of them. I didn't get it and I told them so. These are the opportunities that everyone dreams and talks about. Here someone was opening the door and all were afraid to walk through. It was very disappointing for those of us who wanted it, especially Fred. He was particularly disillusioned. I think he had his heart set on it working out.

For some reason things musically seemed to be going on the downhill. I was starting to get annoyed with Cal. He seemed to think he was the voice of the group. All of a sudden, after agreeing with a booking, he would tell me, "I'm speaking on behalf of the group. I don't think we should be playing a place like that! I think we should cancel."

The place in reference was mob owned, but nice guys who were very professional. They were trying to change the atmosphere of their lounge and felt we were right for the place. I booked and canceled quite a number of times to my embarrassment due to Cal. I finally explained to the owner, Mikey D, as to what was going on and that I was extremely sorry for putting him out and wasting his time. He reassured me he understood and not to worry about it.

Finally I received a phone call from Carlos over the weekend. He was very worked up. He had hung up the phone from speaking with Cal and Patrick before calling me. He was very troubled by Patrick. We had so many gigs and Patrick wasn't willing to give up a job or two with his dance band thereby making no concessions to Summer Knights.

So Carlos took it up with me. "Bobby you've got to talk to them; this isn't right. We need to do something. Maybe we need to get someone to learn all Patrick's parts at rehearsals so we don't have to turn any work down." There were a lot of gigs I was turning down bookings for. I even told Carlos everyone was suddenly getting so picky. When we were singing on a street corner standing over a fiery garbage pail singing, everybody would say, "Wouldn't it be nice to be able to make some money doing this and get off the street corner. " Did everyone forget and want to go back to that!? Carlos agreed with me and I promised to talk to Patrick about it at next rehearsal.

We were rehearsing at Cal's apartment in Coney Island during the week. I didn't bring it up right away- I waited for us to take a break, and then I approached Patrick about the situation. I proposed our idea to a substitute singer. He still was adamant about not giving up any time with his band,

Patrick said, "If you feel like you need a backup, then get yourself another second tenor completely. " I was stunned and taken aback by his response not understanding where it was coming from. I told Patrick we weren't looking to replace him. We just wanted someone to rehearse with us learning his part so that when he couldn't join us we didn't have to refuse any work. Again he came up with the same response.

After no one having ever assumed leadership of the group despite my having formed Summer Knights, Patrick was forcing me to take the position by putting my back against the wall. He angrily repeated the same thing to me over and over, "If you feel that way, get another second tenor."

I paused, took a breath, raised my eyebrows and said, "Well, I guess I'll have to get another second tenor! "

With that Cal chimed in, "If he's out I'm out!"

"Then I guess I'll get another baritone, too!" I fumed. I've never seen such baby crap from grown men in all my life.

With that, Charlie, Carlos and I marched out the door towards the elevator. Down the hallway we walked as Charlie and Carlos told me I did the right thing. "We're with you! " And that they were tired of Patrick and Cal's shit. As we got on the elevator we heard Patrick with a loud drawn out scream from inside Cal's apartment "Fuuucck!"

THE BACK STABBERS

This situation screwed up the works for the group. I had all kinds of gigs booked. Now I had to find and audition a lot of singers to meet and fulfill our commitments in a hurry. There was no time to waste, because we had plenty coming up. As we rehearsed with different people, Charlie and Carlos were never really satisfied with the blend. I had to keep their spirits up and promised them not to worry, that I'd find the right people. I had to be especially reassuring with Charlie. He was always very picky about the blend and the sound, always telling me in his gravelly voice, "I don't know, Bobby," whenever I asked what he thought of a particular combination of new guys with us.

I finally found two gentlemen that I had sang with over the years. The blend was there— we just needed to rehearse and needed time to learn the arrangements. We were just about ready when I get calls at work from both Carlos and then Charlie, telling me they couldn't do it anymore. They were frill of excuses that weren't making any sense. I begged them not to do this to me. I had all these commitments.

"It's just not the same," Charlie kept telling me. Though I had repeatedly tried to reassure him all we needed was a little time and the sound would come, there was no convincing him or Carlos. Summer Knights was over. I had to now break the news and apologize to the new guys. I felt like a damn fool. I knew something was not right. As I made inquiries I found out that behind my back Carlos and Charlie had conspired to go back with Cal and Patrick and replace me! What balls! I was enraged- I wanted no part of any of them anymore. Even as friends. Friends don't do this to each other. Charlie kept calling me leaving me numerous messages begging me that we could still be friends. I never returned any of the calls and never spoke to any of them again.

Subsequently, Tommy from Jump Street called me. "I heard what happened.

"SUMMER KNIGHTS ON JUMP STREET"
Top to Bottom: Tommy Horlic, Cornell Browm, Bobby Monti, Jamie Campbell

Listen, don't worry we're going to make this work. I've got two guys and a girl. We're out as Jump Street again but the girl can't always show. You do first tenor for me as Jump Street and the guys and I can fill for you as Summer Knights and we can fulfill all your commitments." That's how that finally went down. Then Tommy and I had a little tug of war over group names. After everything was done, we dubbed ourselves "Summer Knights on Jump Street," how's that for compromise! I remained with that arrangement until things finally fizzled out for me. It wasn't fun anymore, and it was time to get out.

Things didn't seem quite right at home either. When Dora finished all her schooling for cosmetologist she never did anything with it. All the talk was just a lot of bull. She had plenty of opportunities. A friend of ours had a wedding, photo and limo service. He wanted to put Dora into the package. She had excuses not to. Macy's was hiring for their makeup counter, but there were more excuses from her. She did make up for a couple of women at her friend Don's hair salon, but it never amounted to much. But I knew this. I didn't say anything to her. We were having less and less intimacy. She kept telling me "I know I haven't been a good wife to you. but don't worry. 1 promise. I'm going to make it up to you." I wasn't holding my breath.

My friend Carl called on the phone. You never heard from him unless he needed something. This time was no different. Seems his car broke down somewhere in Brighton Beach. He had it towed to a repair shop. It was in need of a transmission. Carl told me it was going to cost him $ 1200 to fix it. He didn't have any money and begged if I could help him. He proposed to me that if I could pay it on one of my blank credit cards. He promised to pay me back before the following month and interest was due. I felt bad for him. I hesitated, but he swore up and down he would definitely have the money before interest was due. It took Carl the next two years to pay me back ...not even in full and less the interest of course!

As I sat at my breakfast table browsing through the morning papers I saw the advertisements section and said out loud, "Oh my God, look at this! Sons of bitches!" Summer Knights was appearing at Vinnie's restaurant. The bastards hated working there. Now they have the nerve to go back in with the name "Summer Knights." I made that name. That was my group.

If they wanted to go out again, let them make their own bones.

I called an entertainment lawyer right away. I wasn't letting them get away with this. It cost me thousands of dollars to copyright the name. I didn't care. I had my principles and my pride. I had to buy rights legally to the name and then letters were sent out to every member of the group including Vinnie's restaurant and any other place they appeared to cease and desist. It seemed like there was always something to contend with.

YOU'RE MY FAVORITE

In between my busy life. Dora's father asked me if I wouldn't mind helping him paint the living room in his home. Somehow I started out helping him but before I knew it I was doing the entire job. Oh how he raved about how good a job I did and that I was his favorite son-in-law. On and on, that I was his favorite. Seems I'm always everybody's friend as long as I'm doing favors for them. All this love would soon turn to animosity once his daughter filled his head with her many lies. To please Dora we made numerous trips to New Jersey from Brooklyn. She always wanted to visit her family, in between our busy singing schedules. It was very rare that we ever just sat at home and relaxed. She was constantly boasting to everyone how she was trying to get pregnant. We started trying to conceive New Year Eve, thus giving our daughter to be the middle name Eve. That's all she really wanted out of the marriage. At one point I actually told Dora "You have to do it to get pregnant, you know!" Intimacy was so infrequent. She actually stood looking at me stupidly when I told her this, not saying a word, more shocked that I had said something than actually getting it.

Unsurprisingly, after getting married Dora started to find fault with the apartment we were in (her own). She felt we were not getting enough heat for the rent we were paying. She talked about the windows being bad in the apartment. She kept seeing condensation on the glass. I explained to her it was just the difference between the inside and outside temperatures. She was looking for excuses to move. I was starting to see she was the kind of person that tired of things quickly. Suddenly she didn't care about the money and carpeting she had put down from her grandmother. She wanted to move, which became another move with my shelling out money again. We should have kept my apartment on Lake Street, gorgeous, clean, and new. I could even control my own heat. Of course she wouldn't hear of it at the time.

We got lucky, though. and found a great apartment on 11th Ave. and 65th St. in Bay Ridge. It was the entire top floor of a private house with very nice landlords too; they were good people. So I was at it again painting, fixing and decorating.

My daughter Lorrie was now out on her own and living with a fellow named Dustin, who was a little bit of a redneck. She wanted to visit to see me and for me to meet Dustin. She would also be meeting Dora for the first time. I looked forward to it. I hadn't seen her since she came up for a visit when I was with Destiny, a couple of years ago already. They came and stayed about a week. It was nice having them, but sad to see her leave. Dora prompted Lorrie to keep in touch.

During this period of time Dora became pregnant. If I thought I had little intimacy in our relationship, now there was to be none. I know down deep that our relationship was not what it should have been I kept trying to make the best of things and make it work. Emotionally, I was distressed and hurting. I guess being sidetracked with everything that was going on with Summer Knights and moving to a different apartment kept me going.

Dora was about to give birth. She went into labor and with today's technology she was monitored very well. At some point they realized there was something wrong and rushed her into the delivery room. The doctor asked if I was coming in and was I going to be able to do this. I told him I had no problem. I'd seen and been through worse. He was going to do a C-section. I scrubbed up and was ready in the OR. I sat to the right side of Dora's head as they sedated her. When everything was ready the doctor began, I watched the whole process unfold as Dora vomited all over me. It was a miracle to see the doctor pull the baby from Dora's stomach with the umbilical cord wrapped around her neck twice.

I was the proud father of another beautiful girl. We named her Brielle. We had everything to be happy and thankful for. So I thought. Dora kept telling me how she was going to make things up to me. I didn't expect any intimacy after she had given birth. I figured she was tired and her stomach had to heal. We had been looking into building a house in the Poconos as we had already bought land. Dora wanted to go for a ride up there. I thought the baby was too young for the trip, only four weeks old. But, Dora insisted it was fine and she wanted to drive. We had Brielle in a car seat in the front passenger side, with me in the back, leaning over, tending to her. I gave directions to Dora as we went.

There was a split in the road as we're going through northern Jersey. Dora and I were talking as we came upon it, so we were a little sidetracked. I realized at the last minute and raised my voice to Dora, "Stay left, stay left! "

"Oh my God. Look how you talk to me like I'm a piece of shit!' she shouted at me

"What are you talking about? The turn came at the last second; it was just a natural reaction to yell it out to you. It didn't mean anything." She kept going on and on about how she didn't like how I talked to her. It became a full-blown argument over nothing and ruined the whole day. I didn't get it. I was dismayed that she pulled this in front of the baby. I already knew from my first marriage that this garbage shouldn't go on in front of children.

I tried to forget about it as the following week Brielle was getting christened. We did the usual big party in a restaurant. Everything went well. Still I had a sense of things not being right. I didn't know what it was. Out of the blue Dora decided we should make love. I was shocked. I couldn't remember the last time we had relations. It was at least a year ago.

Now I look back at this and have to laugh. I was slow, I was gentle—everything a woman would want. She started screaming like someone was being murdered, "It hurts, it hurts!" I stopped and withdrew myself.

I thought to myself, "Do I look like an idiot! She never even gave birth naturally, she had a C-section!" I didn't say a word. I was hurt at the time, but I laugh to myself whenever I think about this now. Maybe she thought I would spend the rest of my life jerking off!

The following week I came home from work. I saw Dora sitting at the kitchen table wearing what's left of one of my polo shirts. I walked to the sink to wash my hands and take a drink of water. I saw Dora now sitting at the side of the table with her back towards me. "Uhh, Dora, that's my shirt you have on." I said to her.

"Yeah."she grunted.

"You cut the sleeves and the collar off. You didn't even ask me... that's my shirt." I reminded her

She started again with the "look how you talk to me" routine.

"Are you kidding? You take my shirt, do that without asking, and I'm the bad guy?" Of course it escalated. She was bent on not liking how I talked to her.

The next evening I came home and I noticed there was only one place setting on the table. "Aren't you eating with me?"

"We have to talk," she said. I'm sitting down now with her standing over me. She puts on this hysterical crying act "I can't live like this anymore."

I said, looking all around me, "Like this? What are you talking about? You live like a freaking Queen. You don't work we have a gorgeous apartment, what more do you want? You've got it made."

Crying hysterically Dora continued, "It's the way you treat me, the way you talk to me! I can't, I can't!" She would use that phrase in regards to anything, "I can't, I can't!" she kept repeating.

"You know what Dora? There's the door!" I said, indicating the door.

"I don't see anyone holding you back!" The hysterical routine continued as I see her bringing out big brown garbage bags like the ones you use after raking leaves.

"You're leaving in this weather?" I asked. We were in the middle of a thunderstorm while she is going up and down the stairs with the baby in her left arm, and bags of crap she just dragged off the shelves in the bedroom and bath closet. Very important stuff like makeup and toiletries that she shoveled into bags the kinds of things a person such as Dora just can't live without.

She was off in her packed car, along with baby Brielle and her hysterical act in the pouring rain and thunder, headed all the way to Middletown, New Jersey. She announced on her way out she that was going to live with her sister. I let things calm down for a week or two, then called and told her we should meet to discuss things.

We met in a restaurant in Jersey. I told her that her place was home with me regardless of what the issues were and we would work things out. You don't just walk out because you're upset. When she opened her mouth nothing but poison spewed out. She had complaints about more things than I could make up. Me, my family—you name it. She threw it out there.

I sat there fuming. I felt myself flush with heat. That's why I'd meet with her in a public place. I figured I would keep things calm.

But, Dora had no reservations about blurting out everything under the sun. Suddenly she honed in about my family interfering in our lives and wouldn't get off it. She knew she was getting me upset and was keeping it up intentionally. I was sarcastic with her. I asked her how was it that my family interfered when my mother called on Sundays to say hello, but she's on the phone day and night, every single day with her mother and sister and girlfriends. Her answer was, "1 don't know, they just do." What an ass!

A few days later I had a call from her. She told me she was going to come back. 1 figured someone in her family must've told her I was right and her place was at home with me.

She came back for about a week this time, disappearing before I came home from work.

Evidently this was all planned.

She took more loose unimportant things out of the closets, along with some everyday clothing and the rest of the toiletries she missed the first time around. Everything of real importance was left behind. We had doubles of everything, since we had both been single for a while, two toasters, vacuums, TVs, pots and pans. She left all her important papers, documents, birth certificates, (hers and the babies) diplomas, yearbooks. Basically, she left her life behind. It seems it was more important for her to hurt me. She took every dollar she could find, loose change, every nickel, dime, and penny, literally leaving me penniless! She had all my utilities shut down, gas and electric, and phone service. 1 had to wonder what the hell I did to make her this vindictive.

I went to the bank right away after Dora had left I figured I should freeze my accounts of which I was supposed to have had power of attorney, a precaution I took to protect myself from my first wife. As I entered the bank I got looks from the staff and tellers that could kill. To my dismay the bank manager explained Dora and her father had already been there that morning waiting at the door for them to open. She closed and took every account and all funds. I thanked the manager for speaking to me as everyone stared. I could just imagine what Ms. Big Mouth must've told them. As I checked further into my finances, she also confiscated all retirement and investment plans we had properties and all assets. Once again I was wiped out! I was in disbelief!

I went home distraught over my situation while speaking to my mom on the phone. My mother always seemed to have a way of riling me up even more. When I got off the phone I became a madman. Ranting and raving to myself, getting myself emotionally sick and crying to myself. The more I thought about things the more enraged I became.

Thinking all is fair in love and war, this time I wasn't going to be the only one to lose. I started to gather up all Dora's belongings that she had left behind, gathering all her important documents, graduation papers, diplomas, school yearbook, birth and baptismal certificates, just about everything. I started making bundles and placed them at the door. Her toaster, vacuum cleaner, everything we had doubles of, TV set, music equipment, microphone—all went to the curb. If I had a window big enough I would have thrown everything from our second story apartment onto 65th St. and watched the tractor-trailers run over it all!

I spent the evening running up and down the stairs dropping it all in front of the house for garbage pickup. That wasn't to be. The neighbors and anyone that was passing by were having a field day taking things. Out of the corner of my eye I noticed my landlord gaping wide-eyed from behind the living room curtains in shock at what I was doing. Last but not least, Dora's entire wardrobe of which most items still had tags on them, brand-new and never worn or used. On the street it went like a sale at Macy's when they open the doors at 9 AM. When it was all over there was nothing left. Not even for the garbage man!

The owner of the shop I currently work for, Winky told me, "Bobby, I think I'm going to be closing this month. I've got no money coming in. It's not worth keeping the business opened. I know I did a lot of wrong things, I'm sorry! "Winky was a nice guy, too nice to be in business. Everybody was his friend. He'd let people pick up their vehicles without payment with their promise to return. They never did. He had more money on the street than in his pocket. Even though Winky' was a longtime friend of Dora's, I never let him know what had been going on in my personal life with her.

By the following week, that Monday, Winky said, "B, I think I'm going to close this week," and just like that, I was out of work again!

A PRAYER FOR SUNSHINE

I couldn't believe I was going through this mess yet again. I had a second failed marriage, but worse than that I had another daughter I was unable to have contact with. I had hopes for a chance at a new life with a new little family and instead I missed the entire first year of growth of my little Brielle. I spent that year in court fighting for the rights of visitation. My mother kept telling me that she prayed for some sunshine to come into my life. I kept thinking God was punishing me for what I had done years before. My conscience was still bothering me about the wallet in Guam.

I marched down the corridor of the Brooklyn Family Court accompanied by my father. He wanted to be there for support. Dora always had an entourage of family at court. This time was no different. Her father, mother and her sister, who was to testify against me, were all there. My father and I found the courtroom where I was to appear. We both glanced at the door. There hung a plaque of the judge presiding over the court. The Hon. Judge Sunshine! We looked at each other. You know what we were thinking. God works in mysterious ways!

Judge Sunshine had Dora and her family pegged. He listened to Dora tell her story. Then in the middle of her sister's testimony he slammed his hand down on his bench angrily. "Enough," he said "I've heard enough!" He went on, "This is pathetic. You! "He shouted, turning to Dora's sister- "are not even a credible witness. Get out of my courtroom! "She looked at him stunned. "Now! Leave!"

"Are you nuts?" he directed his question toward Dora. "Do you think I don't know what's going on here? I was a divorce lawyer before becoming a judge. Every time you don't get your way you use a restraining order, then milk him along some more, till the next time. I see no reason why this man should not have visitation with his daughter and this court will deem it so! "He set the precedent for picking up Brielle every other weekend, banged his gavel, and adjourned. I had a smile on my face. I had a lot of catching up to do with my little girl. I was ecstatic that I was getting Brielle in time to share her first birthday!

In time to come things would still be difficult. Dora and I were still not legally divorced. She would try to create as much havoc as she could for me. Every time I would pick up the baby, she'd have another complaint to her lawyer. I was always receiving letters of warning that I would in turn hand over to my lawyer. Let them fight it out.

Dora was beyond ridiculous. I would take Brielle out of my car a block away from Dora's home as I returned her from the weekend with me. I did this because Dora's loud voice and her big mouth screaming Brielle's name in the middle of the street would startle Brielle awake and caused her to cry. I couldn't have a peaceful goodbye with the baby. I'd park a good distance from the house, wake Brielle slowly to give her a kiss and hug goodbye and then bring her home.

This didn't sit well with Dora. She actually complained that I was not returning Brielle to her doorstep because I didn't pull up in the car. What an idiot! What's the difference if I drive up in a car, bicycle, or walk up and delivered her to the door. Dora was so stupid she had her father park himself on side street, blocks before I brought Brielle to the door, to see what I was up to. I caught him backing up many times as I passed him on the road. He was another genius! I finally realized where Dora got her brains from.

I had found out that my daughter Destiny had befriended my old friend Carl. She was living with him from time to time. I would bump into them on occasion, just say hello to Destiny, no lengthy conversations. My daughter Lorrie would invite me for weekend stays at her place In Virginia Beach. I'd go and give myself a break from my world of grief. I'd always had a good time there, and Lorrie would tell me "I love you, Daddy", which always made me feel so good.

EPIPHANY

I took a morning off from work. I had an appointment with my divorce lawyer in regards to Dora. I drove down 65th St. As I went through the intersection there were a number of police squad cars with officers in the street signaling for drivers to pull over. Of course I got caught up in it. "License and registration please" I handed it to the officer. He came back to me.

"Please step out of the vehicle."

"Is there a problem officer?" He didn't answer. I got out of the car. "Please place your hands on the trunk of car." Again I asked as he patted me down. "Is there a problem officer?"

He took my hands behind my back and cuffed me asking, Are you aware your license is suspended?"

"No sir, for what?"

"You're in arrears for child support! They suspended your license. Weren't you notified?" I hadn't been. I was still making payments to Lizzie as the court had ordered.

"Well you're under arrest, you'll have to go before the judge and explain yourself"

They put me in the squad car, and I was off to central booking, in jail with all the slime balls. My car was left to be towed and impounded. I explained to the judge that I did not have knowledge that my license was suspended. I also explained that I needed it for work. He said I'd have to apply to DMV for a restricted license.

It was just another way for the system to make money. I paid for towing, impound fees and court fees. My folks came and mom drove my car from the pound until we got home. How ironic that while on my way to my lawyer for proceedings dealing with my ex-wife Dora, I'm still haunted by wife number one, Lizzie!

That evening as I pondered why all these things kept happening to me, I had an epiphany! You know when things are always going wrong we all have a habit of saying why is God doing this to me? I suddenly realized that my God couldn't possibly be still punishing me for what I thought was my worst sin when I was younger, that damn wallet. He wasn't a cruel but a loving God. It was the devil! I realized the devil will stop at nothing to get you to renounce your God! We always wonder why so many bad things happen to good people? It's the devil! The better a person you are, the more he's at you. Why bother with all the slime and misguided fools. He already has them in his back pocket. He's relentless in his quest of the good and humble. He wants to hear them say, "why me, Lord!?" He wants to hear us renounce God!

That evening with that epiphany and tears in my eyes from everything I had endured, I told the devil to go to hell and stay there; that's his home. I will never give up my Lord and I'm ready to die for Him. From that moment on I felt certain calm, all through my life. Perhaps it was because my acceptance of things changed. Bad things continued to happen to me, but my way of dealing with them changed. I tried to stop getting so in a state and making myself sick.

I was in a hurry though, to bounce back from another economic downfall in my life. When Dora left, she wiped me out but the debt was all mine to contend with. I wanted to live well and be myself again. I started dating like crazy. For some reason that always made me feel good about myself, probably because most women actually liked me. I continued to work hard and any opportunity to make more money I was right on it. I had gotten a postcard in the mail about investing in gold that sparked my curiosity. There was a lot of talk about gold taking off. It sounded very enticing. I called and inquired. The agent explained everything to me. I had a lot of questions. It was a plan using leverage, and they would store the bullion. Gold was just under $300 per ounce at the time. I gave him $20,000 of my hard-earned money $10K in cash and the rest on a blank credit card. I was hoping to make a killing, I was making decent money from my job and saw no reason why I couldn't work the leverage plan and the storage fee every month until it took off.

It never happened. It seemed every time I turned around the broker was calling me and asking me for more money to keep the investment sustained at its level. I finally decided it was out of hand; I couldn't keep up with it any longer. It was a losing proposition for me. I was becoming too overwhelmed with all my bills and financial obligations including ongoing lawyer's fees. I was also trying to do the right thing and send money for Brielle. She was still my daughter, even if Porky pig took off with her.

I started making phone calls to the investment company wanting to close my account. Cut my losses and run. Why wait, to lose more money. To no avail I left continuous messages with no return call. Their voice mailbox started having strange messages I was getting an uneasy feeling about the whole thing, wondering what was going on. Finally I got that all-too-familiar "the number you have dialed is no longer in service. Please dial your operator or try again". This was bad! Somehow, one call led to another, I was finally able to find out from agencies in Washington DC that the company was shut down by the government and under investigation for fraud. I found out all pertinent information to putting my claim in with the class-action suit that was in progress.

I was in a mess again. Seems the harder I tried to dig out of a ditch the more dirt I had cave-in on me. I didn't see any light at the end of the tunnel. I buried myself deep again. It was time to claim bankruptcy and start with a clean slate. I always hesitated to do that. Now I had no choice. I couldn't see myself clear on how many years it would take to get me out of the debt I was in. Then still to get on my feet seemed near impossible. As always I never gave up. I just kept plugging along working hard to try to save and get ahead again.

My divorce from Dora was almost finalized. Unfortunately I had set a precedent for child support by trying to do the right thing. I was only supposed to give a certain percentage based on income. What I was sending was above and beyond my legal obligation. Now when I tried to fight it, I told the court I was unable to continue these payments indefinitely, but they didn't want to hear. When the divorce was finalized I saw 50% of nothing. The only thing Dora had to pay me back on was the land I had bought in Pennsylvania. She paid me, not in full of which to this day I have never seen the balance.

On a better note, he who laughs least laughs best. Dora accompanied by her father approached my lawyer and myself outside the courtroom. After two years of not having said a word she wanted to know when she could collect her things.

"What things?" I said to her. "There's nothing of yours in my place. You took everything with you when you left!"

"Oh my God!" she said, "You got rid of everything? What about all my music equipment? Don't tell me you got rid of that too!"

"I don't know what you're talking about. There's nothing there of yours." With a devastated face she glared at me. Her father then butt in, "See, I told you." Maybe she thought my home was a storage area for her crap. My lawyer was impressed with me. He told me he'd never seen anybody so cool and composed in the light of confrontation!

SURROUNDED BY ANGELS

I continued with my journey of getting back on my feet and getting ahead. I enjoyed being single, my social life, and dating a lot of different women. I was seeing a number of very nice girls but I was bored. I felt like I needed something.

I guess it was still that quest for a true love.

I decided to browse through the personals in the newspaper. What an experience! Some women were nice, some weird, and some just nuts! I had connected with a woman named Jennifer. We had many nice conversations on the phone. We were getting to know each other and seemed to hit it off, but every time I pursued us meeting, she had an excuse or reason to put it off. I realized that even though she enjoyed our phone connection she was frightened to death about the process of really meeting with someone. Taking that next step was a hurdle for her,

One Friday evening we were talking and she told me how her mother had stopped by unexpectedly and surprised her. She told me tomorrow was her mother's birthday. She was disappointed she couldn't get out and get her mom a birthday cake to make the day special for her. I told Jennifer I was on my way to spending the evening at my sister's, which would be passing her house on Staten Island. I was willing to pick up a nice cake for her with all the trimmings and happy birthday inscribed on top. I could drop it off to her, meet and say hello. I wouldn't even stay long. She finally agreed to this and asked me if I wouldn't mind picking her up a pack of cigarettes also. This was not a problem.

I knocked on me door to Jennifer's walk-in apartment, birthday cake and cigarettes in hand. The door opened and an attractive dark-haired female peered at me. Then suddenly surprised that I was an attractive man and carried myself well she excitedly exclaimed, "Oh my God, oh my God! Come in! Oh my God."

As I handed her the cake and smokes she apologized for the appearance of her apartment saying that it was small and she was in the process of making changes. It was in incredible disarray. The bedroom was right at the door I walked in from. Her dresser was against the left wall with draws not closed and overflowing with clothing. On top, more piles of cloths and on the bed to the right the same.

"Please sit" she said as she took my coat. I sat on the edge of the bed glancing around the apartment; what a mess! She placed my coat over a chair and came back to me. Standing in front of me she took my hands in hers and again said, "Oh my God! She looked at me and all around me like there were other people there.

"Oh my God! You are surrounded by angels! Not just one or two, you have this aura around you, nothing but angels" she was mystified and I was stunned by her apparition. "Oh my God! So many angels. Come let me make you a cup of coffee." she said as she led me by the hand to the kitchen.

As I walked through the place there were endless piles of phone books with Styrofoam cups on top, filled with snuffed out cigarettes. She had been using them as ashtrays. I looked at the collection of phone books all over the apartment. They were from every borough of New York and every year possible Brooklyn, Bronx, Staten Island, even Long Island. I thought to myself what an eccentric she was as we made small talk and thoughts of her vision of angels filled my head.

As wacky as she was she evidently could see what others could not. I always had strong feelings of angels being with me. This explains a lot to me--why so many incidences of near death in my life when I felt compelled and guided in movements, actions and certain decisions that kept me alive and on the right path. it was another epiphany for me.

We stood in her kitchen. There was no room to sit as we chatted. Jennifer now admitted to me that her real name was Linda. She was afraid to use her real name in the personals. I told her it was okay, that I understood. She began to rinse the coffee pot at the sink. Suddenly gushes of water came pouring out from under the cabinet below the sink. She went immediately into a panic and started crying. I told her to relax, just notify the landlord and he'd take care of it. She didn't want to do that explaining to me he was looking to evict her. She didn't want to give him any more reason. Looking around the place you could see why. I felt really bad. So I told her I would look at it.

"No, no, you're all dressed nicely. I'll figure something out," she protested. "Maybe you want to get a plumber? I suggested

"I don't have any money!" With this she started crying again. I had my everyday clothes in the trunk of my car. I told her not to worry. I changed into my blue jeans and T-shirt. After crawling under the sink I spotted the leak and knew what parts to get. Linda accompanied me to the local plumbing supply store. She couldn't thank me enough. On the way there she told me I amazed her that I had been all dressed and looking so good to switching to jeans and T-shirt and still looking good. That was a nice compliment.

She waited in the car as I shopped for parts. I came out short a few items. I told her I would have to get them in Brooklyn and come back. She'd be without water at the sink for a day. She felt bad and amazed that I would do that for her. I returned to complete the work and told her I would call her.

I called the following week. When she answered she was beside herself, excitedly saying oh my God, oh my God, oh my God! She kept repeating these words so frantically that I thought something had happened just at the moment I called. Linda told me that she was surprised I called. "Well, I told you I would" I'm not one of those people who promises something and doesn't follow through.

I asked her if everything was all right with the plumbing work and herself. It was, and she was very grateful. I told her I didn't think we shared much in common and wished her well. She thanked me again and wished me good luck. It's amazing how God works, how coincidental it was for a girl in trouble to have her sink start leaking and for someone like me to show up to help, fixing the problem, getting her out of a jam. I realized with this incident that, more than the fact that I had angels surrounding me, sometimes, you could be someone's angel, too!

BROKEN PROMISES

I continued to work hard, saving as much as I could. My social life was very active. I enjoyed going out, I enjoyed the company of women, and I realized that all the things you say and promise to yourself to never do again, you will do again. Certain things are personality traits. You are who you are. When events smooth out and the anger inside you starts to subside, you become yourself again. Not that it's bad. It's not healthy to have all that anger and hostility inside you. It eats you up if you let it. You try to learn lessons, letting go of the tragedies in your life and move on. If you don't, you end up staying stagnant. This is what irks the people who hurt you. They wallow in their misery and to see you move on is the greatest revenge of all. It kills them!

I was enjoying having Brielle every other weekend. It wasn't easy with her being out-of-state. I never did understand how the courts allowed Dora to just up and leave Brooklyn with no regard for me. I felt they should have forced her to return to Brooklyn, that was Brielle's home and mine. Needless to say I made the trip. She was worth it.

I was also dating a number of women in New Jersey, enjoying my down time from work as much as possible. But, my having to travel to everyone was starting to get to me and wear me down. I was the only one of my friends and family still remaining in Brooklyn. I was in the center of everyone. I would travel to Long Island to visit friends, Staten Island and New Jersey for my family, girlfriends and Brielle. I was becoming weary of all the travel, thinking to myself, I needed to find a girlfriend in Brooklyn. That would cut down on a lot of my running back and forth.

I would frequent a lounge in Sheepshead Bay known as the Town Café. There was an older crowd. It was a comfortable place to socialize, and most patrons were dressed accordingly. The music was enjoyable, they had a DJ every weekend that played a lot of the music we grew up with, karaoke and a small cozy dance floor to have some fun on. In the middle of dancing with an attractive woman I was bumped by another lady that her girlfriend had pushed into me, done purposely to get my attention. She was a blonde girl that I had noticed in the club, a couple weeks prior when I was there. Evidently she noticed me also. Her conversation with me started with a smile

"You came back!?" We struck up a small talk while we were dancing with other people, eventually leaving them stranded on the dance floor with angry faces. I followed her back to her seat and spent the rest of the evening with her. Her name was Lorrie. I asked if I could drive her home and if I could call her. I was excited about dating her. I was attracted to her and she wasn't the same type of girl I usually dated. She appeared to be more on the serious side and reserved. We started to get involved and a relationship developed.

My daughter Lorrie called, who lived in Virginia Beach, asked me to visit for the weekend. I decided to go. I always enjoyed my daughter's company and had a good time. When I got back, I called Lorrie that I was dating, a few days later. "You don't call to say hello?" she inquired.

"I'm calling you now to say hello," I told her, but she was angry, cursed at me and hung up. I decided to go to her apartment to see her. She hesitantly let me in. I wanted to discuss what the problem was. She evidently felt in a different place in our relationship than I did. She was angry that I didn't extend an invitation for her to join me to visit my daughter in Virginia. I explained to her that my daughter didn't know her and I didn't want to impose as I don't often get to spend personal time with my kids. Lorrie thought she was entitled to certain things already.

She remained angry, showed me the door and slammed it behind me.

Being the person I am, I had to prove to her that I was a "good guy". I let some time go by for her to cool off. Then I called her again. Little did I realize this incident was just the tip of the iceberg? Not knowing the horrors yet to come, I continued my relationship with her. Everything seemed to be fine. She seemed to be easy to be with and we got along well.

I heard from my daughter Destiny. We made peace. She came to visit. We talked and put the past behind. Destiny stayed with me for a week. The weekend came and I picked up Lorrie and introduced them. They seemed to like each other and got along fine. As I was conversing with Destiny, Lorrie out of the blue proposed that she move in with me.

"Really!?" I was somewhat taken aback.

I didn't know if I wanted to do that. All kinds of thoughts rushed through my head. With two divorces behind me I was fearful to go that route in a relationship again. Also I thought of the promises I made to myself. I wasn't going to do it again. I panicked and didn't really answer. I could see the look on Lorrie's face. She wasn't too pleased with my response.

She let me know her anger with me in private. She made me feel like two cents, that I wasn't doing right by her. She made me feel guilty as hell and somehow manipulated me into it just to make her happy. It was an easy move for her. She came with a few bags of clothing, some toiletries and nothing else, leaving her household behind as her daughter Christine lived with her.

Destiny left to go back to Georgia. She was living there now with a man who was the twin of the man her mother was living with. This was a man twice Destiny's age. I asked her what the deal was. She simply stated he was nice. I didn't get it and didn't push the issue any further.

My correspondence with my daughter Eva was becoming much less frequent.

Understandably, she was in her late teens now. I'm sure she was keeping a busy social life and I know school was a priority for her. I myself kept leading a busy lifestyle, finding less and less down time to write. I did miss hearing from her.

I got a call that my mom had a major stroke. She was in Princeton Hospital in New Jersey. I grabbed Lorrie, rushing to make the trip from Brooklyn. We didn't know the severity of the stroke and how mom would recoup from it. When we arrived at the hospital, family members had just left. I introduced my mother to Lorrie as she hadn't met her yet. They exchanged hellos.

Mom was coherent and doing well. We asked her how she felt. She responded that she was tired. We didn't stay long to allow her to rest. Speaking to staff before we left, we were told with pending test results we'd learn more about my mother's prognosis tomorrow. From the looks of things she suffered no major damage and would recuperate well.

We visited again when mom got home, and on one occasion I happened to stop by on my own without Lorrie. During conversation I asked my mother after picking up strange vibes, "So what else don't you like about Lorrie, besides her hair?"

"Well," she responded "I don't really know her. But why did you bring her around so soon? You brought her around too soon."

"What?" I was annoyed. "I didn't know there was a certain timeframe I was supposed to follow." My mother always acted like no matter who I was with in a relationship, I should conduct myself as if I was alone, especially when it came to anything to do with the family such as holidays and gatherings. She'd know I was in a relationship, invite me for a holiday and then tell me to come by myself. She just didn't get it. It put me in an awkward position and annoyed me making me feel like two cents.

Life was starting to become a daily horror. Between my mother and Lorrie, I was beginning to be in an upset frame of mind constantly. My mother continued her negative comments to me about Lorrie whenever I saw or spoke to her over the phone. Things escalated to the point where she started making comments to Lorrie personally, but Lorrie ignored her and never responded back.

As Lorrie settled into my apartment, the true side of her started to surface. She had just lost her job in the medical facility that she worked in for nine years due to a change in administration. She was content not looking for work immediately, taking some time off as a vacation and collecting unemployment insurance payments. Now with time on her hands she spent the days going through my belongings. She'd rifle through everything in my closets, from my clothing to boxes full of paperwork and memorabilia to the contents in my underwear drawer.

When I got home evenings we started to have wars! She questioned everything. She found things that were meaningless and had nothing to do with her, everything I had prior to knowing her. I didn't get what the problem was. She was jealous of people who were no longer in my life. Even souvenirs and mementos of different occasions in my life. She questioned where they came from and more importantly to her who gave them to me

If something was from an old girlfriend she would make me get rid of it. This I did just to stop fighting with her. I finally had it when she ripped a piece of jewelry from my neck. It was my name, Bobby, in block letters, hanging vertically in gold and diamonds. Margarita had given it to me over 10 years prior. Lorrie thought in her sick mind I treasured it for that reason. Who gave it to me had nothing to do with it. I owned the piece all those years and I liked it. It was mine!

Somehow in the scuffle fighting for it, it ended up snapped in half and thrown in the garbage.

Lorrie was really starting to drain me.

Destiny mentioned during her phone conversations with me that she was planning on moving back to New York. She had made arrangements with my old friend Carl who had agreed to share his apartment with her. But, as usual, all was not as it was cracked up to be

A phone call one evening had Destiny on the line, crying hysterically. Evidently whatever accommodations and arrangements she made with Carl were not working out. I knew what was coming as I held my hand to my head. I looked at Lorrie across the kitchen. She surmised what was happening as I listened to Destiny ask if she could come and live with us. I knew what life could be like with her in the house.

Destiny swore it would be temporary until she got on her feet promising to look for work and all the responsible things adults should do. I hesitated in my answer. Lorrie looked at me and said "She's your daughter!" kind of making me feel guilty. With this I realized it was okay with her so I said yes to Destiny.

I picked her up about an hour later making arrangements with Carl to pick up Destiny's dozen or so boxes the upcoming Saturday. I brought Destiny home settling her into what was Brielle's bedroom in the front of our apartment. She'd have to sleep on the floor because I still had the crib set up and no bed.

Lorrie and Destiny got along temporarily. I came home one night after work to a cold and tense house. Both girls were angry at each other. Words and accusations flew back and forth. I had to yell over them to get them to stop and get their attention. The problem was that Lorrie confronted Destiny negatively about her constant inquiries as to what we were doing and what the costs were. Lorrie felt Destiny was up to no good. I stood up for my daughter knowing her inquisitive ways and assuming she meant no harm other than curiosity. I told Lorrie it wasn't her place to confront and reprimand her. If she felt there was a problem she should've related it to me first. Lorrie felt I was wrong but then kept her opinion to herself. I told Lorrie that's the way it is, if she didn't like it she knew where the door was.

It wasn't long though before Destiny was communicating with her ex-beau.

Before you knew it she was making plans to return to him down in Georgia. As quick as she came she left, only staying a few months. Now I had a room full of moving boxes that as usual Destiny would worry about later!

After this little episode with Destiny, Lorrie convinced me to try and straighten out my past. My arrears for child support to my first wife Lizzie had skyrocketed to an unprecedented amount of almost $88,000. Pretty soon they'd be issuing a warrant for my arrest. Lorrie informed me that I could straighten all this out from the Brooklyn courts. I didn't have to take time and lose money by traveling to Florida to appeal to the courts there. I was unaware that I could do this.

So I agreed it was time to try and get my life back on track. I found out I could do this and Lizzie wouldn't even have to appear in court. A date was set and counsel was appointed to me by the court. Of course any time anything is done through the court system it becomes an endless drama. In between cancellations and postponements due to the courts calendar or who didn't show up, the lawyers are late, the magistrate doesn't feel well today, it's unbelievable how anything ever gets done.

Finally with everyone present, my lawyer explained to the magistrate our intentions, which were to clear all added support payments from the time my daughters were emancipated, and an offer of a lump sum payment of that balance to be given to my ex-wife. The magistrate posed this to my ex. With that, Lizzie's response was, "I don't care about the money, I want him locked up!"

"Surely you will never see a dime if I lock him up. He's trying to do the right thing here, what is it that you want?" asked the magistrate.

"I want him locked up! " She repeated. The magistrate looked upward and rolled her eyes, and told me to make a lump sum payment of $5000 and to send payments every month until the balance was paid off. If my calculations were right I would finish with Lizzie about the same time I finished payments for Brielle to Dora. I would be 69. What a sentence! I had no choice, so I made sure to stay on track. I didn't want to fall behind again. Lizzie was right about one thing, as she put it, I was going to "Pay, pay, pay!"

Lorrie started pressuring me to get married. I was very/ hesitant about this since we seemed to have such a tumultuous relationship. I swore I would never do it again. But Lorrie never let up with her manipulating ways. Then I figured if that's what will make her happy, why not? I always figured if a woman was happy, I'd be happy. I was starting to learn that some people are never happy with anything.

I surprised her and proposed on Christmas Eve. She looked at the beautiful ring I got her with disdain and disappointment. I barely got a yes out of her, which was another disheartening moment. She didn't like the ring and we would work on it for the next five years changing stones, cuts, settings and metal. Still she would not be happy with it.

To forgo the expenses and hassles of a large wedding, we opted to go to South Carolina in the spring and marry there with a simple ceremony. We had a small dinner party when we returned, with immediate family in attendance in a restaurant. We both were married a couple of times already and felt this was the best approach.

Now that we were married Lorrie still wasn't happy. She just seemed to become more insecure accusing me of everything under the sun. Every evening when I arrived home it turned into a battle. If it wasn't something she found in my personal belongings, she would check receipts in the bags I brought in from shopping.

I brought home cases of Coca-Cola from the mini-mart across the street from where I worked knowing she liked Coca-Cola. I worked in Bedford Stuyvesant, Brooklyn.

She checked the receipt and said, "Who are you fucking in Mill Basin?

"What? What the hell are you talking about?" The zip code on the receipt was for Mill Basin, so in her mind I was in Mill Basin for an unsavory reason. She fought with me about this. The next day I checked with the manager of the store. He told me they didn't care about the zip code and just punched in any numbers into the machine. I actually had him call Lorrie and explain it to her!

If I came home with flowers for her, she viewed it as I was giving them to her out of guilt over screwing someone. Before you knew it I'd be throwing the vase across the apartment. So many times she placed flowers I'd given her on the table. She'd wait as we sat and began eating dinner. She'd start in: "Who are you fucking that you keep bringing me flowers?" The wars we were having over this. I was starting to become like the animal my first wife Lizzie turned me into.

Like an extreme case of Deja-Vu, we were fighting day and night!

Lorrie would check our phone bills. "What's this number?" reading it off the bill. I didn't know and I didn't recall, but she would continue to badger me.

"Lorrie! Call the fucking number already! Find out who it is." I'd shouted.

She called. It was the Meadowlands Racetrack when once we had called to see when the trotters were running. Now, here's the kicker! The next month the phone bill arrived and we went through all the same argument again because the number she just called showed up again!

One evening in the middle of a battle about God knows what, my mother phoned. Lorrie answered the phone and didn't recognize my mother's voice, became belligerent and hung up on her. "Who's that, another fucking girlfriend? You actually have them calling the house." "You're irrational. That was probably my mother; I was expecting her to call." How embarrassing, now I had to call my mother back and explain.

JUDAS

I went to pick up Brielle. It was my weekend to have her. I got bad vibes as I pulled up to the house. It looked like no one was home. Dora was supposed to have Brielle ready for me on my appointed weekends. I guess she thought I had nothing better to do than to take rides from Brooklyn to Union Beach New Jersey for no reason. I rang the bell, banged on the door, walked up and down the driveway, around the backyard and peered into the windows. There was no one home.

Well maybe she was out shopping and was late to bring Brielle back. I waited and waited and waited. What now? I went to the local precinct showing them my court orders and then I filed a complaint. The staff sergeant told me I'd have to take it to Family

Court. I called Dora's phone a number of times but never got an answer, and I never got a call back after leaving numerous messages.

Monday as I returned from work there it was in the mail: a restraining order from Miss Piggy. Dora was claiming that I was beating and abusing Brielle. I took very good care of my little baby and was always a loving and caring father. This evidently was part of Dora's plan all along to eliminate me from the picture and that child's life.

More court time with endless adjournments, postponements and reassignments. I had constant travel and aggravation as I drove to Freehold's Monmouth County Courthouse. In the process, I found out that my court orders from Brooklyn's own Judge Sunshine had become but worthless papers. Dora was allowed to transfer the entire case to the New Jersey Court system. What a farce to have had documents stamped by the Brooklyn courts with the seal of New York and then suddenly they were meaningless. I was in contact with Destiny and asked her a number of times if she could come and speak on my behalf in court just so the judge would know I was a good father. She would put me off and then tell me she didn't want to get involved between the two cases.

"What two cases, what the hell are you talking about? Would you at least write me a letter then so I can present it to the judge?" Again she made excuses not to get involved between cases. What she was talking about I was soon to find out.

My day in court finally arrived. As Lorrie and I walked through a court corridor on the lower floor of the courthouse, we stepped through the doorway to witness my ex-wife Dora and ex-in-laws in a huddle of some kind. I didn't even want to look at them. Lorrie and I turned and walked the other way to find a way to the courtroom. There sat my mother and father and my sister MaryAnn, all to be witnesses and support for me

The melodrama unfolded. I would represent myself. I didn't have the funds to have my own counsel as did Dora. Her family had money and her sister was very well off. The sister instigated and financially backed Dora. My wife Lorrie and the rest of my family all took the stand, Dora's family too. I question them all and they were crossed by their lawyer

Now the big surprise unfurled. They claimed they had a surprise witness that they had sequestered and would now introduce in court. Their lawyer announced "we ask Lorrie Monti to take the stand."

I was confused. My Lorrie had already spoken. What else could Dora's lawyer possibly ask her? From a side door at the front of the courtroom walked in my daughter Lorrie, all the way from Mississippi! You could hear the gasps from my family as we sat watching her take the stand.

I sat in horror as I listened to the lawyer question Lorrie trying best to destroy my character, with questions of purported abuse to my children when they were young. It was obvious that Dora coerced my daughter Lorrie (and probably paid her airfare) to speak against me. But they were unable to destroy my character.

Finally Dora's lawyer asked Lorrie, "Why are you here today?"

Lorrie broke into hysterical cries, "I don't want to happen to Brielle what happened to me!"

"And what is that?" the lawyer prodded.

"He called me names! " Lorrie exclaimed, sobbing. The lawyer had no further questions for her. The judge then gave me the floor.

"Funny Lorrie, I don't recall that, perhaps you're confusing me with someone else," I said.

She stopped crying and peered at me; she knew what I meant. Without a doubt her mother pumped her with plenty of poison since I left them. She was only 11 years old then and now she was 23

"Lorrie! " I called, beginning my own questions, "How much are they paying you to be here and speak against me?"

"They're not paying me anything," she said, weakly.

"Not paying you! They're putting you up and having you while you're up here!" "No."

"Did I ever spank you?"

"No."

"Did I ever hit you?"

"No."

"Did I ever hurt you in any way?"

"No."

"Did I ever abuse you?"

"Nooo."

"Do you resent me for being a strict father?" "Yes!"

"I rest my case your honor! " I finished.

The judge excused Lorrie from the stand. I watched her walk past her grandparents and aunt, who were seated in the court pews, and take a seat with my ex-wife's family on the opposite side of us as they welcomed her. What a disgrace to speak out against your father in court for a stranger!

It was now my turn to take the stand and speak my piece. I answered all Dora's lawyer's questions, and they were unable to shake or break me.

I explained to the judge, "Your Honor, this has all been staged by my ex, the same way she left the marriage, so she could justify to her parents and peers her reasons for leaving."

The judge asked me, "Do you think your child, Brielle, is lying when she claimed you hit her?"

"Yes your honor. I call it suggestive questioning, Children never want to leave whenever they are to go somewhere else. This is natural. When Brielle was with me she never wanted to return home. When the baby is supposed to be picked up by me and she doesn't want to leave home, it is highly likely that if the mother or anyone else asks, 'why don't you want to go? Does daddy hit you?' you have the power of suggestion to the child, who doesn't know any better, to shake their heads and say 'yes' so they don't have to leave the house. This is especially in the case of a 2 1/2 year old.

"Your Honor, I have already raised three daughters who are all adults now. This whole proceeding is a charade and an attempt to remove me from this child's life. Does it make any sense that the mother places restraining orders on me and now wants to be the supervising adult upon visitation to her residence? What is she going to do, rip open her blouse, dial 911, and I'm in trouble again?!"

"If I am not granted unsupervised visitation, I will relinquish my parental rights." With that, I was done speaking.

The judge countered, "You're putting my back against the wall."

"With all due respect, Your Honor, that is not my intent."

The judge now asked Dora's lawyer, "Any further questions?" Turning to me, he added, "You may step down." The judge ended the proceedings and then announced we would be notified by mail of the court's decision.

A couple of weeks passed, and the court letter appeared in my mail. I was ordered to have supervised visitation in a court facility every other week for an hour with a court appointed trustee. I was disappointed the judge couldn't be a man or a judge and make the right call. He was just looking to cover his ass. After all, I might be a bad man and he'd have slipped up and let me through the cracks.

I called him in chambers. Of course, the judge himself was not going to take the call. A staff member responded. I stated my case and clearly told her to relate this to the judge. "I relinquish all my parental rights. When the day comes that my daughter gives the mother a hard time or she needs help for any reason, I don't want to know a thing. She doesn't have a daddy anymore!

It was no sooner than the visitation case ended that Lizzie had me back in Brooklyn court, looking for more money. As I and my lawyer entered the waiting room, there sat Lizzie with Dora by her side! I turned to my lawyer and said, "Oh my God! "

He viewed the two seated together and sensed tragedy without me explaining. "I'm not even going to ask!" He blurted out. It suddenly all came together for me, the whole thing with my own daughter Lorrie and now Dora in court with Lizzie. It was all a trade-off for information, one big conspiracy with my daughters Involved. They were each and every one of them, all out to get me, no matter what it took.

I could trust no one ever again--not my daughters, not anyone. All the "I love you!" salutations I got from my daughters and "Daddy, why don't you come spend the weekend?" with Destiny asking questions and sending information back to her mother. What a plot!

They'd been setting me up for years. Even my wife Lorrie was right, pegging Destiny about all the questions. There were ulterior motives to it all. I was devastated that they would all plot against me, and I was angry as hell.

Lizzie got nowhere in court. Any information Dora had became completely useless. During my marriage to her, I had everything in Dora's name, including ownership of my insurance policy; she had taken it all when she left me. Dora walked away with everything. These two women manipulated everything and everybody, gaining nothing in the end.

The ones to suffer would be my daughters, as I would never see or hear from any of them again. I received a letter shortly after the court proceedings from Destiny, but I was so angry I never responded other than to send back her boxes which I had been storing at my apartment. I never even wrote to my daughter Eva. I just figured, along with the rest, she had become her mother's daughter. I never heard from her again either.

My life kept spiraling out of control. I continued to battle with my wife Lorrie on a daily basis. Stress and hostility had become a way of life for me, even in this third marriage.

My mother called me and told me to come to Jersey. She needed to talk to me. She and my father were worried about leaving their inheritance to me. My mother expressed concern that she had dreams of Lorrie walking off with whatever I had achieved again and that she was with me only to use me for money. This all might have been true but I didn't need to be running to my parents' home to hear about it. I had enough problems under my own roof to deal with.

My mother made sure she expressed her displeasure with Lorrie whenever she could, especially every time we were together. She would make snide, cattie, insulting comments right to Lorrie's face. Lorrie would ignore her and not respond- Now my mother wanted to know why Lorrie refused to go to a particular family function. My mother expressed desire to patch things up between them. I told my mother if that was the case then she should call Lorrie and speak to her. I also told my folks I didn't give a damn about their money or anything else, and if they were so worried then they should remove me from their will, which they did!

Later that week as I arrived home from work Lorrie greeted me with, "Your mother called today."

"Oh, how'd that go?"

"Not good. She asked me why I didn't want to go to the family party. I told her I didn't feel comfortable. She wanted to know why, so I told her she's been insulting me and saying nasty comments to me for the last couple of years. I even asked her what was with the card she gave us for our wedding, 'Good Luck Son', with no mention of the bride. Who gives a card like that? I didn't even know they made a card like that. She wasn't too happy about my answer to the question. She called me an Irish bitch. I hung up on her. I don't have to put up with that shit! I'm not even Irish!"

Oh this was great and just what I needed—more grief. I called my mother and told her I thought she was looking to patch things up and not to make the situation worse. She started to complain about how Lorrie ignores her even when she calls to say hello. I was confused and asked my mother, "What the hell are you talking about?"

She went on to explain how Lorrie brushed her off and looked to get me on the phone right away. I told my mother, "That's a lie because I'm usually standing right there when Lorrie answers the phone. I hear her response to you. She says hello, how are you and everybody? Then you ask to speak to me, and I hear Lorrie say he's right here. If you want to chat with her, why don't you, instead of asking for me?"

My mother insisted she was right and aggravated the daylights out of me. The fact that this whole incident took place on the phone was ridiculous. But she kept right at it until I finally told my mother she was a liar.

She responded with, "I want all your things out of here: your car, your boxes, your belongings. Anything I've given you I want back. Good luck with your life! "With that, she hung up on me! I thought this was so petty! Now here she was, disowning me! She always had to be in control, and God only knew she was always right! I felt like I was in a constant state of agitation.

I had enough problems of my own to contend with. Life with Lorrie was a continuous nightmare. The next day I received a call from my sister MaryAnn who wasn't too happy with what I said to my mother, shocked and saddened to be honest. I kept referring to her as "your mother" as I spoke, which seemed to aggravate my sister even more. I know my sister did not understand what had taken place the last couple of years between my mother, me and Lorrie. I'm sure the picture my mother was painting to everyone wasn't the whole story.

That was the last phone call I got over the incident until the following month my dad called, his tone very cold and serious. He was letting me know that my mother wanted what she asked me for, and he wanted to know when I was coming to take my things. I arranged it with him for that following Saturday. I went to my parents' home and was coldly received. I took my Chevy out of the garage and any boxes of my belongings that I had, emptying their home of any traces of myself.

I didn't bring the items she wanted, I felt they were mine. When you give something to someone, it's not yours anymore! Dad intermittently called the next few months insisting I return whatever she wanted. Tired of hearing it I made a special trip out to Jersey to drop them off finally. I asked my mother what her problem was; what had Lorrie ever done to her? She didn't respond to that, but only spewed out more nonsensical venom.

"We've entertained enough of your girlfriends over the years. I don't want anything to do with her or her bitchy bastard kids! "My mother spat. Then she brought up my ex-girlfriend Margarita's boys. Once, when mom had us for dinner, she asked them if they wanted second helpings, and they said yes. The boys finished whatever was on the table, and my mother had no leftovers. It obviously irked her! That incident was 15 years before!

As far as Lorrie's kids being entertained, my sister had us for Easter and I had asked if Lorrie's daughter Christine, who was an adult, could join us so as not to be alone. My sister had no problem with this but evidently my mother resented it. I wondered since when was a Monti table ever bare, especially for a holiday? It was always *aborndanza* and a feast enough for an army!

I awoke the next day distressed and in disbelief. My mother never had us over for dinner as a couple, nor did she ever entertain Lorrie's children. I would not hear from my family again for the next three years. My brother wouldn't acknowledge me for the next five. My father finally called while I was at work three years later. I returned his call later that evening, and we agreed to get together. When we did, no one mentioned a thing. It was awkward at first, but we continued to act as if nothing happened. I guess it's best to leave the past behind you when you want to move forward.

ICING ON THE CAKE

During those years life was a nightmare, taking the cake as the horror of all time for me! I worked my ass off trying to save money for Lorrie and me to have a good life. I devoted my time doing everything and anything I could to please her and make her happy. I tried to be the man every woman would want as a husband. I gave her all the love and attention I could. I tried to buy her happiness spending thousands and thousands of dollars on jewelry and fine things for her. I showered her with love and affection and all the best money could buy. I even spent over $40,000 on dental work, fixing her lifelong overbite and distorted teeth that she was never happy about, so she'd have the most beautiful smile in town. Still she wasn't content! She wasn't satisfied with her engagement ring, so we were always working on that. If I bought her a beautiful piece of jewelry, she didn't care for it, and I'd have to return it for something else. Whatever she did desire was always an upgrade, costing me more and more money.

I bought her a drop-dead gorgeous piece of jewelry for Valentine's Day. This was one-of a-kind piece that was custom-made. I took an entire year struggling to pay it off. When she opened the box she looked at it and said, "1 don't like it. You KNOW I only like diamonds'

I was so upset and hurt I said something that was out of character for me but I wanted to hurt her back, "Give it to me; I'll give it to my girlfriend!" Of course, a war ensued after such a statement. She was always accusing me of affairs anyway. I felt so hurt, I just didn't care anymore. Even the jeweler was stunned in disbelief when I returned it. This piece got changed for a diamond tennis bracelet with emerald cut diamonds.

The accusations and innuendos were a daily way of life. I picked up Lorrie from work and she'd notice that the vents in the car weren't in the same spot they were the night before.

The seat wasn't the same. Who was in the car?

Sometimes I would drop off one of my coworkers at the train station after work. I had to account to Lorie for everything and every minute of my time. She'd look at me accusingly, asking, "Where did you get these napkins from? " They were a different design than she remembered. I tried to keep some in the car with her in mind.

"Lorraine, they're ours. I took them out of my lunch bag from home She'd insist they weren't and we'd keep fighting.

On a winter's day, we'd walk across snow getting into the car. She'd reach down and touch the floor mat and say, "How come it's wet?"

"Lorraine, you just walked through the snow, didn't you?" She'd insist it was wet from before even though I was home all day!

After coming home from work and coming out of the shower, I'd see Lorrie holding my underwear, pulling them out of the hamper. "Why are your underwear all stained?" she'd ask suspiciously.

"You're kidding me, right? You've forgotten we were intimate before I left for work this morning. I was late and I just jumped into my clothes and ran out the door! "Everything and every day was a fight.

We were having sex one night and she stopped in the middle of things. "What's this hair on you?"

"It's probably yours," I'd sigh.

"No, it's not mine!" she'd insist.

"Well then, maybe it's mine! "

"No. it's a long hair and it's not blonde!"

"Lorrie! It's probably mine; my hair is long in back. When it uncurls the hair is long!

Needless to say, that would be it for intimacy that night. I learned never to get out of the shower, towel dry my hair first and then the rest of my body, because I might get a hair stuck somewhere!

Speaking of having sex, that was another horror. If we didn't have sex sometime during the evening and then again at bedtime and then again before I left for work in the morning (making sure to repeat this day in and day out without ever taking a break), then this meant I didn't love her. Even Superman needs to rest!

Having sex with Lorrie was like making love to a mannequin. She was lifeless. I became terribly stressed and hateful of her that I had to think of other women in order to keep going. This was something I never had to do before. It didn't matter if she was exhausted; all she had to do was lie there. She killed my ego. Being we were both tired, yet in her mind I should prove my love for her, she would actually fall asleep while having sex. It was demeaning to me as a man. Making love had become a chore, an obligation, rather than the want of it!

One Sunday the pipes under the bathroom sink started leaking. I crawled under to fix it. I was greasy and dirty but I needed parts, so I went off to the Home Depot on Third Avenue. When I got home. I found Lorrie looking at the time of checkout on the receipt while she questioned me where I was.

"Lorrie, it takes a half hour to get back home from there!" I tried to reason.

"I don't know about that!" She insinuated in her typical way that I was up to something.

"Lorrie, look at me—I'm filthy, and I'm trying to fix the sink so we can have a decent Sunday together. What'd I stop for, a blow job! Give me a break already!" Of course, it didn't stop and I crawled back under the sink.

I got dressed one Saturday to bring her to work. She was bartending in a lounge. "Where did you get that shirt? I never saw that before. Who gave it to you?" she started with her Inquisition.

"Lorrie, it's been in the closet. It's an old shirt I haven't worn in a while," I explained.

She kept insisting someone gave it to me. It turned into another full-blown battle she kept repeating, "Who gave it to you?"

"So what do you think, someone gave it to me as a gift? I walked in the door one night, hid it from you, and then I hung it up? With all the times you go through my things you never saw it hanging in the closet? It's been there since you moved in." Her badging continued as I drove her to work.

Like the ass that I am, I used to give up my Saturdays to spend time with her in the lounge where she was working. There was only one patron there when she opened. She served him a beer as she set up shop. She waited and then the moment the patron left his stool and went into the men's room, she started, "So Bobby, who gave you that shirt?" I was annoyed; it was the straw that broke the camel's back. I tore the shirt off in Hulk Hogan-like fashion. "Here's the fucking shirt. Lorrie!" as I tossed it at her face, "Happy now?" I stormed out of the bar enraged and shirtless.

I couldn't take anymore. It was getting to the point that I wanted to kill her. I was starting to become afraid that I was going to hurt her. I suggested to her that we seek counseling. She refused. Her answer was there was nothing wrong with her. It was me that had a problem. Oh yeah, I had a problem all right, she was my problem!

I decided to go on my own and continued for the next year. Lorrie would accuse me of getting worse since I was going to counseling. The truth was she was getting worse, and I was just responding to it. She fought with me until I promised not to go back to the therapist. I agreed with her and went anyway. I needed to find out why I kept hooking up with the same type of women. Fighting continued. I threw her out on numerous occasions only to take her back again. She would always promise me she would change and things would be different. Somehow she knew how to manipulate me, but the dysfunction continued. I started leaving the apartment during the fights. I couldn't take it. I started sleeping in my car and not returning home for days at a time.

Then when I came home we'd fight some more, because she never believe I stayed in my car. There had to be some woman putting me up! Geeze, it never ended.

I found a 24-hour gas station with the little bodega inside. It had facilities if I needed to use the toilet. I was a wreck living like this. I'd dress and undress in the backseat of my car and go to and from work. I wasn't eating right and started to become very sick from all the stress. I knew I was going to have to change my life somehow. I needed to start looking for a place to live. I also rented a van, and with the help of one of the mechanics from work, I removed a lot of my treasured belongings out of the apartment while Lorrie was at work and put them in storage.

Through all of this discourse I was still going to the psychologist. I believed that helped me tremendously. I had no one else to talk to, no family, and I didn't want to burden my friends. My friend Mike called me one day at work, and I couldn't help myself I broke down and started to cry, "How the fuck do I always hook up with these psychopaths?!"

Mike was very concerned about me. He kept repeating, "What's her problem?" I was too choked up to talk. It was all so complicated. How would anyone understand?

I told Mike of my plans to move, and he suggested I get out of Brooklyn and look in Long Beach. We used to hang out there and sing years ago in our teens and we always loved it out there.

He told me he was looking and knew a few of the agents. I told him I would think about it.

My relationship with Lorrie was growing worse and worse, if that was possible. The longer I stayed away the more she kept accusing me of being with someone else. We had come out of her daughter's apartment after visiting one evening. Lorrie decided to rifle through the glove box of the car before we pulled out of the parking spot. I just knew she was going to find something to make an issue over.

"What's this phone number?" She found a name and number on a loose piece of paper. It was the information from a guy who had rear-ended us on the Belt Parkway he was a foreigner and had one of those male names that could be mistaken for a woman's.

Of course, Lorrie didn't remember. We battled in the car. I got so verbally loud that passersby stopped and peered at me. I was enraged. I lowered the window and told them, "Be smart, mind your fucking business!" I was in a state I could very well have hurt anyone and not cared about it.

I realized Lorrie had shoved me over the edge. This was not the first time she had me yelling at other people. I just couldn't take it and be with her anymore. She kept refusing to leave, as much and as often as I begged her to get out of my life.

Again, I started living in my car and living on a staple of Chinese food. I had to find a place to stay. Living in my car was making me more ill. I was in such a terrible state even my boss put me up in his home one evening, offering more time at his house if I wanted. But I hated imposing though I was appreciative. My leave of absences from my home and Lorrie were beginning to go from days to weeks.

A real estate agent I had met in my search for a place to live called. She knew I was in a bad situation and was willing to make some calls for me. She found a place that was basically a starter for people who were down and out in Williamsburg. Cheap rent and a roof over my head would work until I could get my act together.

I took a room there out of desperation. The room was actually a cubicle amongst three hundred, a 4 ft. by 6 ft, cell, if you will. It was enough for a cot and a small closet with no ceiling above. Beside people like me who were down and out, the place housed what seemed like every low life degenerate one could imagine. There was a unisex bathroom facility that gave me skives from the get-go; there was no separation of men and women in the building. As I entered the bathroom I was greeted by the remains of a woman's period on the floor, disgusting shower stalls, and unflushed toilets full of excrement, urine and vomit. I was disgusted to take a shower and wondered if I'd get hot water. Surprisingly, I did.

I knew I'd have to do whatever it took to survive here. After I cleaned up, I went out to get some basics such as soap, towels, and toilet paper. I padlocked my door when I left, as I saw most people do. The element here could not be trusted. I spent many a pensive hour here as the next few weeks passed. I occupied the last cubicle on the top floor toward the back of the building.

Aside from the fact there were people playing radios and music through the night, I couldn't sleep with the emergency exit light peering over my head into my eyes. I needed to rest, so I climbed up the wall hoisting myself above the two-story window and unscrewed the bulb every night. I guess as they made their rounds every day, the custodians would correct it. As disgusting of an experience as this was, my time spent in contemplation brought me to another epiphany as to why I kept hooking up with the type of women I did and getting myself into these situations.

When I was a young boy, my father would always tell me "whatever you do in life, be the best you can be." That's what I always strived for. I found myself trying to be better than everyone else. If someone got upset with me, I had to prove I could do better, be better, or be the best. This belief existed in my life since childhood.

I strove for perfection for my mother, the nuns in grade school, and carried it into all my relationships. All the girls I dated and had mini-relationships with who were happy with me, I was fine with because they accepted me for whom I was and didn't feel the need to prove myself. The women who gave me a hard time, found fault with me, or who were never happy with me were the ones I got drawn to and hooked on. It seemed the more they had a problem with me, the more I had to stick around and prove myself. That was it! I kept looking for that approval that I never got. That's how I kept getting involved with the wrong partners. Now I needed to recognize the signs and avoid them from ever happening again.

I finally started to realize that some people were never happy. No matter what you did for them, it was never good enough. But in truth, they're not happy with themselves. Never knowing what they want, how could anyone else know? They're just miserable human beings.

BEGINNING OF THE END

I knew I had to get out of this awful place I was living in. I started looking on Long Beach like Mike suggested. I saw some really gorgeous places--magnificent condos over-looking the Atlantic. The more I saw the more I realized I deserved to live this way—a better life. I owed it to myself with all the years of suffering and hard work.

I saw an ad in the paper for a brand new condo that was just being completed. I spoke to Mike about it. He told me he saw it himself, and it was everything the article said it was, plus he knew the agent and he would hook me up. I went to take a look. I was sold. I fell in love with the place. But (and there is always a "but") the condo was beyond my means. They were all million dollar apartments.

The apartment I was interested in had an asking price of about $900,000. There was no way I could even come up with a down payment. I had also made arrangements with a mortgage house in Manhattan. They were advertising on the radio and offered incredible plans. Michael's real estate connection, Joyce, was the key for me to get in.

Lorrie suddenly showed up at my work place one day, surprising me as I turned from my work bench. Apologetic and begging me to come home, she took a cab to the shop. I didn't say much. I knew I couldn't take living the way I was in a box in Williamsburg. so I returned home to her.

I announced to her that I had filed papers for divorce. All she had to do was sign when I got them. She was upset to say the least, and begged me not to do this. As usual, she promised things would be different and that she would change. I told her that was wonderful, but I still didn't want to be married to her anymore.

She said, "Bobby, please, I'm begging you, don't do this!"

I told her, "Show me change and we can still be committed without a piece of paper." She knew nothing of my plans to leave, and that is what was in the back of my head, which was to be able to leave with a clean slate and to not be legally bound to her.

In the process, though, she found out my intentions. The agent from the mortgage company in Manhattan called when I wasn't home.

I had given him strict instructions not to call since I didn't want Lorrie to have any knowledge of the transaction. His message was that something needed my immediate attention and was important. With the cat out of the bag, now Lorrie wanted to know everything. She begged to be a part of it all. As usual she poured it on and manipulated me to give in. I don't know why I just never could be strong and pull away from her. However my lawyer sent the divorce papers in the mail addressed to Lorrie. She was upset to say the least trying to get me to agree on her not signing them. Somehow I finally stood my ground with her and insisted she sign them. I convinced her we could stay committed without the legalities. 1 guess I was able to stand my ground because I never really wanted to marry her to begin with. I was only trying to make her happy, which it didn't anyway. She knew I was moving to Long Beach with or without her and if she wanted to go with me I think she felt no choice but to sign the papers.

It killed her but she signed!

In speaking to Joyce, the real estate agent, I told her there was no way I could manage the price they were asking. She said, "Robert, tell me what's in your mind."

Even with all the money I had showered on Lorrie during our time together, I still had the 10% they needed.

50K in cash. I could take out a 10K loan on my insurance policy, and I had just gotten another 10K personal loan offer through one of my credit card companies. I offered 700K on the condo as I had 70K for a down payment, or they needed. I'd be doing this by the skin of my teeth, but Lorrie promised to help.

Joyce said, "Let me see what I can do." I got off the phone with her and figured there was no way they would accept an offer that low. A half hour later the phone rang. "Robert, it's yours!"

I couldn't believe it. I was so excited. I was already contemplating the thought of selling down the road. I figured this would be a great investment for me and would fund my retirement. The way the market was moving I figured in five years the place would probably bring 1.2 or 1.3 million. This would be a major profit of a half mil for me. I could live comfortably along with whatever else I socked away in that time.

Joyce recommended her lawyer to me who also happened to be the DA of Long Beach. I got in touch with him immediately and got the ball rolling, I brought him the down payment that went into escrow and then also told the mortgage house in Manhattan to finalize their paper work. Of course, my now ex-wife Lorrie was on her best behavior for the move.

About six weeks later I got the mortgage contract papers in the mail that I was supposed to sign. Oh God, I was in shock! The payments would be almost triple of what they had originally quoted me. I called the firm and had a verbal war with the agent. They had scammed me to get me in. I was signing nothing and called my lawyer in Long Beach, begging him to get me out of the deal. We had a problem. He explained there is a clause in the contract called "time is of the essence" meaning in not so many words that if I reneged on the deal after the set time period, I stood to lose my 70K down.

I couldn't believe it! This was my life savings at this point, and everything I had. I couldn't afford to lose it. My lawyer reassured me. If he couldn't straighten things out with the present mortgage company or get me out of the deal, he'd find someone else to get me in. That's exactly what he did. Of course, rates were not what I originally had planned on but not as high as the Manhattan firm had given to me.

It was going to be a struggle. My lawyer assured me not to worry; he'd set it up so that I'd have 35K cash out at closing. "Make a few months' mortgage payments in good faith and then we'll refinance when things settle," he instructed.

So that was the deal. We made the move. I struggled with the mortgage and taxes that were costing me $6,000 a month. Lorrie was doing me a big favor by paying the $345 maintenance fee for the month. Every once in a while she would throw me a twenty dollar bill for gas in the car, since she refused to get a job in Long Beach.

I had to travel to Brooklyn three nights a week to pick her up from the lounge she worked at. I took the Long Island railroad home from Bed Sty, showered, get cleaned and dressed and then leave to drive to Brooklyn at 9 p.m. She'd stop working by 10 p.m. By the time we got out the door and got home, it was 11 p.m. Then we'd start to cook dinner. I waited to eat with her, because I thought it was nice to eat together and the right thing to do.

The condo was beautiful with all amenities such as a high-end, exclusive lobby and secured staff with concierge desk. It was a thrill to realize how the other half lived. Now we were the other half, but living beyond our means. I struggled to make payments. Every penny I made went out the door. I explained to Lorrie that it was costing me $300 alone just to pick her up from work every month. This was not just gas to Brooklyn, but two bridges with tolls. I wasn't getting a cent more out of her.

With each month came a mortgage statement from a different company. They kept selling the loans. I was going broke and pressed my lawyer to get refinancing going. I kept trying to convince Lorrie that there were plenty of places in Long Beach she could tend bar. The area was nothing but restaurants and lounges. But she refused. She didn't want to lose her customers. She didn't get the concept that the clientele in Long Beach was a different class with more money in their pockets. I'm sure she would have done better in tips and salary.

The longer we settled in, the more Lorrie returned to her jealous and insecure ways. I was hoping life would change for the better. I even got a canary when we moved in. My friend Dean who I worked with raised canaries, and his home was full of them. Dean gave me the bird as a gift. I dubbed Dean the "Birdman of Brooklyn." I thought having the bird would contribute a peaceful ambiance to our apartment. I named him "Broadway." He was always singing. He loved to sing along with my old Doo Wop records and was crazy for Tony Bennett. I would tease, "Broadway, do you want to be a Doo Wop singer?"

As hard as I tried to keep it together, life was just getting harder and more stressful. Lorrie and I were at odds with each other constantly. Every attempt to refinance had become in vain, with even my lawyer giving up. All of a sudden the entire economy was crashing. I was on the string of my teeth financially. I had gone through everything I had. I looked endlessly into all organizations supposedly offering help to those in crisis.

I wasn't the only one. The government and local civic groups had all kinds of gatherings and meetings with political leaders and bankers seeing people on a personal level. I exhausted every avenue possible. I started believing that the majority of these efforts were for show politically or for the media's and public's perception. There was no help for anyone.

There were no more options left but to put the place up for sale before I went into foreclosure. I was a mess. The stress was killing me. I left one morning, driving into Brooklyn. I had a 2 p.m. appointment at the VA hospital for a checkup with my primary physician. I left work early. On the way the phone rang. It was Lorrie.

"What? You don't answer your phone unless it's the normal habitual time?!"

Once again she was on the warpath as I was driving to the hospital. I didn't know what the hell she was talking about. "I was trying to call you all morning."

I asked if she had the right number, because my phone never rang. She started accusing me of being with a woman. Of course, we had a verbal war, and I hung up on her. By the time I got to the hospital, my blood pressure was sky high. I checked my phone. I had gotten one call from Lorrie as I was in traffic on Atlantic Avenue. I never heard the phone. I was in traffic with tractor trailers shifting gears next to me. I had my music playing in the car and my phone around my waist under my winter jacket.

I explained this to Lorrie after sitting in the car waiting for her after the VA Hospital in Brooklyn from 5:30 p.m. until 10 0'clock to bring her home. We fought as usual all the way. I asked her what was so important that she couldn't leave me a message. She persisted with the usual lies about how many times she tried to reach me, but she was always right and I was, of course, up to no good.

I flipped out in the car as we drove down Emmons Avenue in Sheepshead Bay. I stopped the car dead in the street, got out cursing and yelling, and told her to find her own way home. I was extremely keyed up. As I turned and looked at her through the window, she was laughing at me, enjoying it all. I took my phone and threw it on the ground, smashing it into pieces. This was all over a fucking phone call! With all the anger and rage she brewed in me, I again yelled at people passing by to mind their own business. I think I was at a point I could have killed someone.

I was getting sick to my stomach. My life was a nightmare in progress. There were no takers on the sale of my condo. I started contracting with different real estates, and short selling was becoming the big option. There was no money anywhere. People were losing their jobs. No one was buying anything.

The following week I had another huge battle with Lorrie. This one took the cake. I picked her up from work. As we started to take off in the car she told me, "I met your friend Frank today at the Flatbush station. He told me whenever you take the car to work or the VA, you pick up Barbara and take her with you!"

I ride the railroad into Brooklyn from Long Beach with acquaintances from town, Frank and Barbara. I told Lorrie it was nonsense and a lie. I never did that even though Barbara worked not two blocks from my job. I couldn't understand why Frank would say something like that. I thought perhaps Frank did say this to Lorrie, thinking he was being funny. He was a prankster and joked on the train with us in the mornings. Not knowing what Lorrie was like, he could have possibly said what Lorrie accused him of saying.

I was distraught. No matter what I said to Lorrie she didn't believe me, which upset me even more. I told her, "You believe a stranger over me?" We battled all the way home. I didn't sleep all night. I had myself worked up. I was going to kill Frank. Evil visions and thoughts were going through my head.

First thing on the train the next morning, I approached Frank. "You saw my wife yesterday?" He looked at me cross eyed with a "huh?" look upon his face. "You bumped into my wife on the Flatbush station?" I asked.

"Nooo, Bobby, I haven't seen your wife since the antique car show last summer. Why? is everything all right?" I turned and sat taking a seat with my back facing him, shaking my head. "You okay, Bobby?"

I couldn't even answer him. It was a lie Lorraine made up to see if she'd catch me at something. I had another war with her that evening. I called her a liar and everything else under the sun. "Now you bring other people into things! This is how people get killed for no reason!" And I'd be responsible for hurting someone who had nothing to do with anything! I told Lorrie, "You're a fucking idiot!"

She turned me into an animal. It wasn't over yet. Her story, (or her lie) Lorrie insisted, was true. According to her, Frank was lying. She had to save face. We argued about this for days, finalizing on the balcony that Saturday. I told Lorrie, looking down at her as she reclined on her lounge chair, "The things you do to me. You should thank God you're a woman, 'cause if you were a man, I'd fucking kill you!"

She responded with a casual, "I don't think so." That was it, I snapped. I was out of control. I started yelling at the top of my lungs, "You piece of shit! I'll throw you off the fucking balcony. You think I care anymore, you think I care about these people?" I screamed as I noticed the entire beach crowd had stopped.

Our condo was right on the beach. Everyone was watching and listening.

Everyone on the street stopped. I looked at the crowd as I yelled out, "These people don't give a fuck for me and I don't give a shit about them. You think cause your here you're a better person? You're shit! Lorrie, you forget, I was in the military? I learned how to kill people. Do you think I'm so easygoing and nice that I can't hurt someone? Never mind the streets I come from in Brooklyn and the gangs I dealt with as a kid! You know nothing about me! "

I left her there reclining in her chair. The air between us became permanently thick. The tension and coldness in the house was sickening. Sleeping and living in the second bedroom became my new way of life. We did nothing but avoid each other weeks at a time. Yet I still maintained the routine of picking her up from work. We just never said a word to each other anymore on the ride home or once in the door.

My longtime friend Mike and Marie invited us out for a visit to their home in Oakdale Long Island. The weather was beautiful, and we hadn't seen each other in a while. They were aware of life between Lorrie and me but never said anything. I didn't elaborate too much when Michael would ask me about things. He was always baffled and said, "What's her problem?" He knew me a long time and knew the kind of person I was

Lorrie and I put on a good face and headed out to visit. We sat in Marie's solarium having cocktails and kidding with each other attempting to have a good time. Michael mentioned something about being in the doghouse and I added that at one time I was in the doghouse so often that the guys at work had posted a sign on my locker, "Doghouse." We chuckled.

Lorrie asked "who were you in the doghouse with?" My stomach turned right away and I knew there would be hell to pay. You had to watch every P and Q with her. It never took much to start her. I turned to her, "Not you Lorrie! Guess I'm going to pay for that!"

"Yeah, later," she replied.

I was on pins and needles the rest of the day. We weren't in the car but two minutes, ready to head home when she started. "So who were you in the doghouse with? Huh Bobby? Answer me! "

"My first wife," I braced myself.

She yelled back at me, "Why don't you fucking go back to her! It's the same shit over and over, you keep thinking about these other women!"

"What are you nuts? Everybody had a laugh. It was a JOKE! " she kept badgering and I started to palm her head with my hand telling her to shut the fuck up.

"We can't even visit people, have a good time and leave happy, you miserable bitch! " She was swinging wildly back at me as I was driving. I knew we had to stop. I had to get us home in one piece. We ignored each other the entire ride home. We walked in the door, and I went in one bedroom and she went in the other. That was it! I had enough, this was over! I had to get rid of her before I hurt her. I knew Lorrie was not worth my spending the rest of my life in jail.

We didn't say a hello to each other for the next three months. It was difficult to go on living under the same roof with someone when there's so much tension. We sat at the table one night, and I was going to propose something to her. I knew what the answer would be before we began, but I had to ask.

"Mike is offering to hold the mortgage in the short sale, if we come up with the cash. If we short sell for $500,000 we would have to come up with $50,000. He would make the purchase in his name and after we were on our feet again he'd turn it back over to us in our name. So the place would still be ours. Your name could be on the deed then too, What do you think?"

"I don't have any money!" she said. If I have $9,000, it's a lot"

"Lorrie, you must think I'm stupid. You've been working for years. I know what you've earned. Even if I bottom-line it, you should have way more than that saved. You've given me nothing over the years. I've paid for everything—food, clothing, and shelter! "

"I don't have any money!" she insisted.

"Okay Lorrie," I was annoyed, discouraged and upset. I was annoyed not because she didn't want to do it, but because she lied about everything. "You know what? We were never a team, a partnership, a couple. It's always been 'what can Bobby do for Lorrie?'

That was the most we ever spoke. Two weeks later after having spoken with Mike and telling him the results of my conversation with Lorrie, I asked him what he thought I should do to get her out of my life. I told him I wanted to take legal action if I had to. I couldn't continue like this. He suggested I write her a letter so there would be no confrontation telling her what I would do.

So, that's what I did. I wrote Lorrie telling her I wanted her out by the end of August or I would take legal action. Then I got smart. I just didn't care anymore and knew I had to not give a damn about her, her safety, or how she got home from work. This was the catalyst that got her ass finally moving. She realized I wasn't going to do things for her anymore. No more stocking her favorite wine or cases of Coke in the house. No more buying anything. All the things I did routinely for her whether we were arguing or not, I stopped doing.

The biggest thing of all that ended was not to go to Brooklyn to pick her up from work. I was tired of not being appreciated. Now she had to take the subway from Sheepshead Bay to Atlantic Ave., connect to the Long Island Railroad and into Long Beach and pay for a cab home. She was coming in after 2 a.m. in the morning. The following week I spotted her daughter dropping her off so she was home the usual time. But that didn't last too long. Her daughter wasn't about to make a two-hour trip every night and then go to work herself the next day. I guess not everyone is Bobby.

August rolled around with no maintenance money from Loraine or a peep out of her. She waited until the following week and then she told me, "I'll be out by the 15th!" I didn't say anything.

I had to come up with the rent money myself. Two weeks on the house for her! It was typical Lorrie behavior and petty to me, so I didn't make an issue out of it. Then I mentioned to her, "Lorrie, you see everything here in this apartment?" She looked at me. I went on, "It belongs to me. I better not see anything disappear!" She took me seriously for a change. I was tired of losing all my belongings to women that used me.

Coming up with extra money for me was a challenge. Lately my boss was starting to play games with me. He would send me home or tell me to stay home so he could save the day's pay. This went on every week. We had a conversation about it. He told me he was carrying me since the transmission end of the business was slow. I told him it seemed to be okay with him when all we had was transmission work, and I carried the shop! The conversation led nowhere. I knew he intended to continue with evading paying me my salary, and I was starting to see the writing on the wall. He knew my situation. He wasn't going to get rich on saving a day's pay here or there, but he didn't give a damn. It was about him and the almighty dollar.

At last came the day for Lorrie to be out. Her daughter Christine came to help her with her belongings. There were no goodbyes as I sat on the balcony peering out at the beach. Christine only approached me with some manila envelopes for postage. She asked if I would mind forwarding any mail her mother might receive. I told her okay, and I saw sadness in her eyes. I couldn't tell if it was for her mother or for me.

Lorrie was already waiting for Christine in her car. I heard the door close behind her as I was still peering out from the balcony. I was distressed yet relieved. The tension in the house would now disappear. Even Broadway had stopped singing. I never felt as empty and low as a man. Lorrie had done such a number on me.

STARTING OVER

I was so emotionally jarred. I felt like she smothered me and robbed me of my being. I had no sense of self and no self-esteem. My self-worth and dignity were gone. I felt like a lost animal. How will I ever be Bobby again, I wondered? I cried for myself. I knew I needed to go on, and feeling sorry for me wasn't going to cut it. I prayed as I always did for God and my angels to help me through.

Finally with help from above, a wonderful young couple viewed my condo. They loved it and a short sale deal was in the works. I told my friend Mike the good news. He was very worried about me. He reminded me to start saving some money as I didn't even have enough to move out.

"What are you going to do, where are you going to go? Back to Brooklyn?" he asked me.

I didn't know. I had been so filled with anxiety that I wasn't thinking clearly. I needed to get some good sleep and regroup. A return to normalcy in the house with no one fighting with me was the peace I needed. I started to prepare to pack and move out. I would be putting my entire condo and all of its contents into storage, This alone was breaking my heart. I had tried so hard and in vain to make a home here.

I picked myself up and knew I had to persevere, continue to work hard, and get back on my feet. I did it many times before. Now I must do it again. I couldn't dwell on the fact of how tired I was.

I headed in to work as I always did. It was Veterans Day and I thought to myself, I should be off today. Nobody is working and this veteran is going to work. It was freezing out but the sun was blaring down. As I arrived in front of my job, I noticed the large garage door to the shop was wide open. As I entered the building I was muttering sarcastically to myself, "Here we go, another day with the door wide open. Just because the sun is out we think its springtime!"

Little did I realize my boss had been outside his office and overheard my muttering? "Go home, you have an attitude, go home!"

He just loved sending me home so he could save some money. You'd think I had nothing else to do but get up at 5:30 in the morning to take the Long Island Railroad into Brooklyn so he could say go home.

"You know what? If I go home I'm not coming back. I've had enough of your shit. Yeah, I've got an attitude. I'm tired of freezing my ass off at work while you sit your office like you're in Miami!" He said nothing further. I knew this was it. How nice to do this to me on Veterans Day. I walked to the back of the shop and locked up my toolbox. I'd have to go back to Long Beach, get my car and then drive back into Brooklyn to get my tools. I wasn't worried. I was usually able to get a job before the day was out without even bringing my tools home.

This time was different. I was in for a big surprise. It was like the world was caving in. There was no work anywhere. The economy had collapsed beyond anyone's wildest expectations. Shops were in the midst of closing down as I was going in to ask for work. Where there were once three rebuilders in a single shop, now there was only one. The bosses were hanging on for dear life that their businesses would survive. People were being laid off like crazy.

I would take the Yellow Pages with me. I started to search in all the boroughs. I would get to places only to find empty buildings. It was unbelievable! Now I was really in a fix. No wife, no home, no job, no money. I didn't want to tell anybody in my family. I didn't want to have them help me. I was still too proud. What on earth was I going to do? I didn't give up. I kept up my search for work every day.

Mike called and made me an offer, "Bobby, why don't you come down here to Florida. I have a spare bedroom in my condo. Take a little time to relax and recoup. Look for work down here. You can make a fresh start, a whole new life and get away from the cold weather once and for all."

I decided to take him up on it. I had his wife, Marie's blessing also; otherwise I wouldn't even have considered it. I never liked to impose, but I didn't have many options. I had saved up just enough to make the move. I would truly be starting from scratch again.

I didn't realize how bad things were until I ran out of food. My regular monthly bills never ceased to come either. In order to survive I started selling off assets I had accumulated over the last few years. Knick knacks, collectibles of all kinds, rare stamps, almost my entire coin collection, complete sets of rare silver dollar coinage and all my silver jewelry. This is what would sustain me until I was out the door. I managed to hang onto my gold jewelry. That would be a last resort.

As far as food, I had not a penny left to feed myself. I found out where the local food pantry was. It became my fine dining experience for the duration of my stay in Long Beach. I appreciated it with all my being. I was only too glad not to be starving in the streets. They would also send me home with bags full of leftovers to carry me through the evenings. I hungered every morning until the pantry would open at noon. Every day I thanked the Lord for giving me my daily bread.

It was extremely hard to believe all this was happening at this point in my life. I should've been looking toward retirement; instead, I was starting over.

I remained busy with preparations to go forward, finalizing any business I had in New York. I made a last visit to the Brooklyn VA Hospital for a checkup and made sure all was in order including my records and medications.

This was going to be a major move for me, heading to Florida with nothing. I went into the chapel at the hospital to pray and asked for God's help. I broke down as I knelt and prayed. I was so distraught. I sat in silence for a while viewing the walls in the chapel. There was Jesus in the "Stations of the Cross" falling and getting up, falling, time after time and getting up again! I was having another epiphany. Maybe Jesus was sending even more of a message about life and not just that he died for our sins. Maybe this is what he was showing us: life is falling and getting up endless times. If we are strong and persistent we can also arise again. It's amazing what you can read into things. Maybe my guardian angels were guiding me to see this. It made me feel better to realize this.

The closing on my condo went smoothly. I wished the young couple well. I reminded them to love and be good to one another, and they would have a wonderful life there together. They were set to move in for the first of April.

Ironically, I would be arriving in Florida on March 17, St. Patrick's Day. I thought to myself "I hope this is a good omen." Maybe with a little luck my life would change.

I watched as the movers loaded the last of my belongings onto the truck, leaving my home empty and barren, silent and surreal. This was my life!

The awkward evening laid itself down on me. I prepared a spot on the barren bedroom floor, spreading a quilt down that I could wrap myself up in. I sat Broadway's cage down beside me. Then I stacked my clothes for tomorrow under my head as a pillow. I was exhausted. I laid myself down on the quilt feeling the cold hardwood floor beneath me. I made myself as comfortable as could be. My mind wondering to thoughts of a bright new future . . . 1 knew with my faith in God and help of my Angels I would bounce back, if just one last time. In the pitch blackness of the night I closed my eyes "I guess it's just you and me now, Broadway! " I whispered into the dark.

Suddenly, I heard a calming voice echo, "you are not alone!" My heart jumped as I saw a vision of an angel kneeling on one knee in the far right corner of the bedroom. He was in an aura of gleaming gold and orange. Breathtakingly beautiful was this vision! The rays of light illuminated the room. I lifted my head and opened my eyes. ..There was nothing there. Stunned and confused I laid my head back down. Again, the vision and the voice said, "You will be blessed now with the Holy Spirit to give you strength in your journey, as you go forward."

The vision faded. I felt a heated rush going through my body. It melted me into serenity. I closed my eyes and drifted away into the magic night...

SUMMARY

96 Tears is tribute to the human spirit. When all seems bleak and the mind sinks to lows it thinks impossible to handle, the heart and soul remain the substance of true character!

Being Destitute, broke, down and out, near death experiences...used, used and abused, only then do the magical, mystical forces of faith come into play....This is the driving force that lifts us up from the depths of the darkest places our mind and bodies take us. This is a story of never ending perseverance, the song the heart and soul sing to never, ever...ever give up!

ABOUT THE AUTHOR

Bob Monti is a rare breed, not because he is the only person to have faced trials and tribulations in his lifetime, but because he has kept his dignity and pulled himself up by his bootstraps over and over and over again.

His book is testimony to how much pain and loss the human spirit can endure; he has always risen to meet his next obstacle with a strong will to survive. His positive nature is an inspiration to others who find themselves faced with seemingly insurmountable obstacles. Reading his memoir reminds others that perhaps "this too shall pass" in their own lives.

Bobby has settled and permanently resides in Naples Florida. He continued to persevere in his daily life. After many more years of numerous situations, his perseverance, faith in God and strength of character, have blessed him with abundance, peace, harmony and Love in his life.

Those that know his life story well have often remarked that he needed to write a book. Bobby accepted that challenge and set to work with this memoir. This book proves that the old adage, "Truth is stranger than fiction" is certainly true!

MaryAnn Miano

AUTHOR
Robert Monti

www.ingramcontent.com/pod-product-compliance
Lightning Source LLC
LaVergne TN
LVHW042244070526
838201LV00088B/18